Praise for *The Dre*

A lifelong study of the music of Johann Hasse by conductor David Wilson has culminated in his superb new book, *The Dresden Manuscripts: Unearthing an 18th Century Musical Genius*. Hasse's music achieved great popularity during his lifetime, only to be overshadowed later in history by other composers, especially Mozart.

Dr. Wilson's important and illuminating focus on the Dresden manuscripts will certainly be a springboard for conductors and musicologists to further examine the entirety of Hasse's oeuvre to rediscover other gems, particularly among the masses and operas, many of which will be found worthy of reentering the repertoire.

David Wilson has produced a revelatory work of refined scholarship that will deepen our knowledge of this important yet oft-neglected Baroque composer.

Morten Lauridsen
Distinguished Professor of Composition
USC Thornton School of Music
Recipient, 2007 National Medal of Arts

THE *Dresden* MANUSCRIPTS:

UNEARTHING AN 18TH CENTURY MUSICAL GENIUS

To Elizabeth,
Best wishes

THE *Dresden* MANUSCRIPTS:

UNEARTHING AN 18TH CENTURY MUSICAL GENIUS

David Wilson

THE DRESDEN MANUSCRIPTS:
UNEARTHING AN 18TH CENTURY
MUSICAL GENIUS

Copyright © 2014
by David Wilson

cover design by Lucy Swerdfeger

Cover art: the Hofkirche by Canaletto, circa 1748
(This image is in the public domain.)

Published by

NEW EDUCATION PRESS
Scottsdale, Arizona

Paperback ISBN: 978-1-932942-80-7 — $ 19.95

E-Book ISBN: 978-1-932842-81-4 — $ 9.99

NewEducationPress.Com

Published in the United States of America

Acknowledgments

I have carried this story in my head for decades. If it hadn't been for a casual remark a friend made one evening, I may never have put it down on paper. That friend turned out to be my publisher, Dr. Steven Swerdfeger. Thanks to his support and encourage-ment, I found the time and motivation to write my first book. The journey began as a research project, and I have both Dr. Novak in Vienna and Dr. Reich in Dresden to thank for their invaluable assistance in helping me locate the materials needed to complete my dissertation. I am also indebted to University of Illinois Professors Charles Hamm and Harold Decker for serving as mentors and advisors for the project. Their example of pedagogy and scholarship inspired me. I owe a debt of gratitude to John Daleiden, Moderator of the West Valley Writer's Critique Group, for helping me find my voice as a creative writer. As my previous publications were in academic circles, his critiques and those of the group wisely guided me through the editing process. To Camilla Wilson Scott, who in every way has been my muse throughout this entire journey, and to my sons Scott and Brett, whose love and support has enabled me to attain goals I never thought possible, I owe more than words can express. As with the dissertation, I respectfully dedicate this book to the memory of my parents.

ॐ   ॐ   ॐ

The author cordially invites you to visit his website, where you will be able to hear the concert described in this book as well as to find additional links of interest.   **http://djwilsonauthor.com**

Table of Contents

Prelude

The final chords of the "Amen" echoed throughout the immense nave of the *Kreutzkirche*, the post-war spiritual home of the people of Dresden. I froze. I did not want to lower my hands so I could treasure this feeling for as long as possible. Although I had conducted hundreds of concerts, this one was deeply personal. It represented the culmination of a dream nurtured for decades. I had just brought to life a work not heard for almost two hundred and fifty years. I wanted to savor every moment.

Someone shouted *"bravo"* and the spell was broken. The applause which started as a ripple began to swell. Before turning to acknowledge the enthusiastic audience, I humbly bowed to the choir. They could tell by the tears in my eyes and the smile on my face how proud I was of their magnificent performance. We had come halfway around the world to give this concert, and the enormity of what we had just accomplished was overwhelming. Judging from the looks on the faces of the singers, I felt they shared the same emotion.

As the performers filed out, I retreated to the sacristy behind the altar. I could not stop the tears. As I wept, I began to reflect on how this journey began, a myriad of images flashing before me as vivid now as they were some thirty-odd years ago when I first embarked on this adventure.

Thinking about that moment now, I had so wanted my dream to end differently, but fate was not so kind.

Chapter One: Genesis

Both the humidity and temperature were over ninety on that sultry day in June of 1966 when my journey began. Drenched in sweat, I tumbled out of my trusty Mustang onto the tree canopied campus. After a hectic three day drive, I was eager to get out and stretch my legs.

My car didn't have air conditioning. Who needs it when you live on the West coast? It didn't even have a radio to help me while away the tedious hours of the hurried trip from California to Illinois. What a dumb idea, I thought, but at the time a luxury I could ill afford living on a high school teacher's salary.

Not having bargained on the muggy heat, I opened the door and it hit me like a blast from a steam room. Even though hot and tired, I was excited to be in this small mid-western town in the middle of nowhere to join the throngs of those waiting in line.

I parked my car in the gravel lot behind the Armory, an immense barn-like structure home to the ROTC. Today, it served a different purpose—the site of summer school registration.

After an hour of waiting outside in the numbing heat, I was ushered inside. Signs, arrows and helpful people guided me through the maze of tables and desks confronting me.

I had come all this way to embark on a long cherished dream—to begin work leading to a doctorate in conducting. Although the path to this decision was arduous, it had been embedded in me since I was a child. As long as I could remember, I felt music had chosen me and I had chosen music as my life-long career, a career I would passionately embrace and would take me all over the world

The registration line inside the Armory inched forward, giving me plenty of time to reflect on the importance of this moment. Like a slow-motion video, scenes from my life flashed before my eyes: a small boy sitting at his mother's knee listening to the Saturday morning Met Opera broadcasts; an eager fourth-grader grasping the clarinet for the first time as the teacher patiently guided his fingers to cover the holes; a boy soprano singing "O Holy Night" at a Christmas Eve service; a teenager shaking hands with Dimitri Mitropoulos, legendary conductor of the New York Philharmonic; a nervous adolescent auditioning for the junior symphony; a cocky high school senior conducting the orchestra when the teacher was ill and the sub didn't have a clue; a proud junior touring the country with his renowned college choir; a naive student teacher demonstrating Kodaly hand signals to not so eager fourth-graders; a graduate teaching assistant wracking his brain to find ways to engage jocks in an "Intro to Music" course; a first year high school teacher winning a superior award at a state music festival; an enraptured conducting student lunching with Aaron Copland at Tanglewood, the summer home of the Boston Symphony; a brave young conductor presenting a concert in Vienna with a choir and orchestra he founded; and finally, a nervous applicant opening a letter informing him he had just been admitted into one of the premiere choral conducting programs in the country.

"Next," someone shouted, shocking me back to the present. An attractive co-ed led me to a table where the Dean of Graduate Studies was seated. A distinguished looking man more round than tall with shoots of silver in his dark, wavy hair patiently guided me through the steps necessary to matriculate as a new grad student. I filled out a myriad of forms, selected my courses, and paid my fees.

At the conclusion of the process, the Dean handed me my admissions papers, a class schedule, and a campus map.

School would not begin for several days. I had plenty of time to check into the dorm and familiarize myself with the campus. Having received my degrees from a small liberal arts school of fifteen hundred students, the immensity of the University of Illinois campus, with an enrollment of over forty thousand, was at first look daunting. It resembled a small city, completely self contained.

I moved into graduate housing, a multistoried building not far from the Armory, then set out to familiarize myself with the campus and find where my classes would meet. After accomplishing those goals, I planned

2

to spend the rest of the day in the library. I was on a mission. I wanted to find music written by a composer who had piqued my interest several years ago.

According to the map, the School of Music was now temporarily housed in several old mansions until the multi-million dollar Krannert Center, complete with concert and recital halls, offices and classrooms was built.

I walked along the sprawling lawns of the central quad, past the campus center, and around the ivy covered administration buildings. The heat was stifling. I stopped to wipe the sweat from my brow. In the distance I saw tall cranes, the construction site of the new Music Center. I headed in their direction.

Several blocks later I came to a cluster of gracious Victorian homes, the temporary site of the School of Music. With wrap-around porches and gabled roofs surrounded by stately elms and oaks, these mansions would be my academic home for the next eight weeks.

After locating my classrooms, I returned to the main quad and headed toward the library, a large, imposing, three-story brick building fronted with Romanesque arches and cascading steps. The Dean mentioned something about the music library being temporarily housed in a labyrinth of rooms in the basement.

With great anticipation, I climbed the library steps, entered the immense marble foyer and descended the stairs leading to the lower level. The elegance of the entrance, its polished marble floors and tall latticed windows, soon vanished. I found myself in a dark narrow hallway. Feeling my way along, I spied a door labeled "Music Library" in large gilded letters and entered.

Passing through the reading room, lined with shelves crammed with over-sized books and music scores, I went directly to the reference department where the card catalogue was located.

My eyes focused on a single drawer I hoped would end my search. Labeled HAM-HED, I pulled it out, found a tall stool and sat down. With a pad and pencil in hand I thumbed through the well-worn cards, certain at any moment the rich contents of the U of I music collection, reputed to be one of the largest and most complete in the world, would answer my questions.

What was I looking for? Anything I could find about an obscure 18th century composer by the name of Johann Adolf Hasse. I first encountered his name several summers ago while searching for music for my high school girl's vocal ensemble. I had received a fellowship to study conducting at the prestigious Berkshire Music Festival in Tanglewood, Massachusetts, the summer home of the Boston Symphony. One of my conducting teachers, Dr. Iva Dee Hiatt, was legendary for her work with the Smith College women's choirs. I asked her about repertoire suitable for my girl's ensemble, and she inquired about the music they had performed. When I listed several titles, I could tell she was impressed.

"I have just the piece for you," she said, "a lovely yet challenging work by Hasse, his *Miserere*."

I confessed I had never heard of him, but was intrigued by her suggestion.

When I returned home after that inspiring summer, I read all I could find about this composer who was new to me. There wasn't much. A short article in the *Grove's Dictionary of Music* stated Hasse wrote the *Miserere*, a setting of Psalm 51, for the *Ospedale* in Venice, an orphanage for girls who were trained to become professional singers and instrumentalists. Many famous composers, including Vivaldi, wrote works for this institution. In addition to the *Miserere*, the article mentioned Hasse composed masses, operas, oratorios, requiems, symphonies, concertos, chamber music, solo cantatas and sacred works. He was indeed prolific.

I was intrigued and purchased the music Dr. Hiatt recommended. I made an arrangement for strings to accompany the choir and presented Hasse's *Miserere* at the Spring Concert. The girls loved the music and so did the audience. The beauty of Hasse's compositions, his soaring melodic lines, his rich harmonic language, was apparent to all. From this brief introduction my curiosity was piqued. I wanted to find out more about this composer whose music I liked but knew so little about.

Sitting at the table in the Music Library, I thought all I had to do to end my search was thumb through the card catalogue, find reference numbers, go to the stacks, and find a treasure of Hasse scores. I had done my homework—knew his dates (1699-1783), where he lived and worked (Dresden, Vienna and Venice), and how prolific he was.

Hasse, along with Handel and other composers of his day, enjoyed an international reputation. He was called *Il divino Saxone*, (the beloved Saxon), *Padre del musica*, (father of music), and his fame was renowned throughout the capitals of Europe. I had no doubt the immense collection of the Illini Music Library would have hundreds of his works, and I would have a field day studying them over the course of the summer. Today, I just wanted to get an idea of what was in the library and make some notes.

My fingers flipped through the cards. I spotted one familiar to me, a reference to the piece I had conducted with my girl's choir:

Hasse, Johann Adolf (1699-1783) "Miserere in C minor"
(Psalm 51) for SSAA, soli; piano, vocal score ed.
by Hugo Leichtentritt, (New York, G. Schirmer, 1937).

Turning to the next card, I was shocked. There was another composer's name in the heading. Where were Hasse's other listings? Frantically, I searched for other references, but discovered this was the only one. I wondered if cards may have been removed for cataloguing or to add more entries? But the drawer was full. There was little room for additional cards.

What to do next? I picked up the drawer and went to the reference desk in the next room. A youngish woman, her brunette hair tied up in a bun with a pencil stuck in it, was busy at her desk. She looked up as I approached.

"May I help you?"

"I certainly hope so," I said, explaining my dilemma, hoping to hear an easy explanation. She assured me all of Hasse's scores which the library owned would be referenced in the card catalogue.

"If the library holds other works by Hasse, you would have found references to them in the drawer you are holding." There was such a sense of assurance in her voice.

"Could someone have removed any of the cards while doing research?" I sheepishly asked.

"That's not permitted" she retorted.

"Let me check the Master Catalogue and see what I can find," she said while disappearing through the door behind her desk. Minutes later she returned.

"Sorry to inform you, but the card catalogue is complete and up to date. There is only one reference to your Mr. Hasse."

Not believing my ears I stood there for several seconds, a stunned look of bewilderment on my face. Muttering a weak, "Thanks for your assistance," I slowly walked back to the catalogue room and returned the drawer to its rightful place. There had to be some mistake, some logical explanation. I was determined to find the answer.

Little did I know I was about to embark on a great adventure, one which would not only take me behind the Iron Curtain, but would require decades to puzzle out.

Chapter Two: Reflection

My next encounter with Hasse was three years later. During that time my life had greatly changed. I completed two more summer sessions at Illinois, accepted a position as choral director at a community college, married Camilla, the woman of my dreams, completed a four week European concert tour, and now was attending a lecture in Vienna as part of an International Choral Conductor's Symposium, my new bride by my side.

One of the most noted lecturers at the Symposium was Dr. Leopold Nowak. As curator of the music collection of the *Nationalbibliothek*, the Austrian State Library, he was responsible for the preservation of music written by Vienna's most famous composers. Original scores of Haydn, Mozart, Beethoven, Schubert, Brahms, Bruckner and Mahler, just to name a few, were housed in this library.

After a fascinating lecture on the care of these priceless autographs (original scores in the hand of the composer), Dr. Nowak invited the class to visit the library where he would show us some of these treasures. To my surprise, just a handful took him up on this generous offer. Many said they had been in class all day and wanted to get some rest before the evening's concert by the Budapest String Quartet.

I was tired too, but something inside told me not to pass up this unique opportunity. I leaned over and whispered to my wife, "Honey, we should go." As a superb musician and violinist, her curiosity was as keen as mine. She readily agreed.

From the Academia, where the Symposium was held, we boarded the tram for the short ride to the *Hofberg*, the winter palace of the Hapsburgs, the ruling family of the Austria-Hungarian Empire. The *Bibliothek* was nestled among the old royal apartments which now house several museums.

The outside of the library was non-descript, but when I entered the foyer the splendor of the original palace was revealed. Polished marble floors and staircases, elegant Baroque mirrors, crystal chandeliers and massive paintings proclaimed the wealth and power of the Hapsburg dynasty. For a moment I imagined I was about to meet the great Empress Maria Theresa herself.

I snapped back to reality when Dr. Nowak instructed us to leave our personal items with the attendant in the adjoining cloakroom. We were not allowed to bring anything into the room where the priceless manuscripts would be displayed. Ordinarily, this room is not open to visitors. Scholars must have a letter of introduction and a valid reason for viewing original manuscripts, making this opportunity even more extraordinary.

After depositing our things, we rejoined the Professor who led us into the main reading room. With its high barrel-vaulted ceiling, black and white marble floors, tall narrow windows, and rows of tables with individual reading lamps, the room was a most impressive sight. As access time to the library is limited, researchers were taking full advantage of this window of opportunity. This fact would be made clear to me several years later when I returned to do my own research. For reasons known to no one, Vienna's two most important libraries were only open at the same time—Tuesday and Thursdays from 1-4. The room hummed with activity.

We were ushered down a narrow hall to the Rare Book Room. Guarded by an imposing metal door, we entered and sat down at a large table in the center of the small windowless room. I felt closed in, like I was in a vault. Dr. Nowak introduced the reference librarian, a rather plump, middle-aged woman with extra-thick reading glasses and a stern look in her eye. She instructed us on the proper protocol of viewing these scores.

"Before you touch any of these priceless manuscripts, you must put on these gloves," she demanded, as she handed a pair to each of us.

For the next several hours I sat spellbound as masterworks I had studied and loved were unveiled: Brahms' *4th Symphony*, several Schubert art songs, Haydn's *Lord Nelson Mass*, Bruckner's *Te Deum*, and fragments of the Mozart *Requiem*.

Dr. Novak then handed a large well-worn manuscript to my wife. I could see tears welling up as she reverently opened the score— Beethoven's *Violin Concerto*, a work she had spent much of her life mastering. But this wasn't a published edition. She was holding Beethoven's original manuscript.

That's when it hit us. We were actually seeing the original hand of these composers, not facsimiles or reprints, each manuscript revealing so much about the composer himself. Whereas Mozart's hand was immaculate, clear and vivid, Beethoven's score was confusing, full of rewrites, crossed out measures, erasures and scribblings. Mozart heard the entire work in his head before he wrote it down, further testament to his prodigious talent. Beethoven, on the other hand, agonized over every tortured measure, as evidenced by multiple versions of the same motive scribbled in the margins.

What a wealth of knowledge was revealed by studying these autographs. With each score Dr. Nowak added anecdotes about their unique properties, the state of research, the most authentic modern editions, the most reliable editors, all priceless information for any musician. I made mental notes of his comments so I could write them down once back in our hotel room.

At the end of the presentation, Dr. Nowak asked if there were any questions. I was bursting to ask him about Hasse, but waited until he answered questions posed by other students.

Finally, I inquired if he knew of any music by Hasse. With a twinkle in his eye he questioned why I was interested in such an obscure composer. After I shared with him my brief encounters with Hasse, he said if I could stay a few minutes, he would answer my question. I agreed and began to speculate on what he might tell me.

After the students left, he disappeared for a few minutes. When he returned, he carried two large nondescript boxes in his arms. He placed them on the table, opened the largest one, unwrapped its content and handed it to me. To my complete astonishment, it was a score by Hasse, his Requiem Mass dated 1763. Here was the first evidence I had of his music other than the *Miserere*, the piece Dr. Hiatt had told me about and that I had conducted several years ago with my girl's choir.

Hesitantly I turned the brittle yellow pages to get an overview. Some two hundred pages in length, the score was for orchestra, soloists and chorus. At first, I was struck by how much the music resembled Mozart's, and made a mental note, not knowing at the time how significant that observation would prove to be.

Although like Mozart's score, the manuscript was clear and carefully written, Dr. Nowak was quick to point out it was not an autograph, but a copy made sometime in the late 18th century.

"Most scholars agree," he went on to say, "that few autograph scores of Hasse's music now exist due to two cataclysmic events—the bombardment of Dresden in 1760 by Frederick the Great, and the firebombing of Dresden in 1945 by the Allies at the end of World War II. Either catastrophe could have destroyed the majority of Hasse's music."

Had he just revealed part of the puzzle? The reason I couldn't find any works by this elusive composer in the Illini library?

The other box cradled a Mass by Hasse, dated 1751. Again Dr. Nowak reminded me the score was a copy not an autograph. Nevertheless, I now had further evidence of Hasse's music. So far this brief encounter had convinced me that not all of Hasse's music had vanished.

I thanked Dr. Nowak for his kindness and vowed to return to the library someday to study these works.

I was taken by surprise by his next comment.

"I know you have no time now to study these scores, but if you come back tomorrow, I will have a letter of recommendation for you which will assure you access to the library next time you return to Vienna."

I was overwhelmed. His name alone would open doors, and I would join those elite few who were permitted to view these priceless scores. Another piece of the puzzle was now in place!

After the Symposium, my wife and I flew home, packed up our belongings and drove to Illinois. I had been awarded a teaching assistantship at the U of I and would now have the time and resources to be a full-time graduate student. No more summer sessions for me. Camilla resigned her elementary music teaching position. I took a leave of absence from the college, and we both raced off to embrace another new opportunity.

ॐ   ॐ   ॐ

The next two years were crammed with teaching assignments, classes, papers, exams, rehearsals and concerts, all requirements to compete course work leading to a DMA (Doctor of Musical Arts) in conducting.

Having conquered the last of these hurdles, it was time to schedule the final written and oral exams, nicknamed the "dreaded qualifiers" by my colleagues. Only after passing these tests would I be allowed to write my dissertation, an exhaustive study representing original research which contributes to the field.

In addition to studying for the "writtens," I had to settle on a suitable dissertation topic which must be presented in some detail to my committee at the conclusion of the oral exam. But there was one catch—my "orals" could not be scheduled until I passed the "writtens." A lot was at stake. If I failed the "writtens," a definite possibility in my mind, I would have only one more opportunity to retake them. Failing to pass a second time would result in my dismissal from the degree program. After years of arduous work I would walk away with nothing but a hollow feeling in the pit of my stomach and would join the countless throngs of those who tried but failed.

Rumors abounded about the difficulty of the exams from my colleagues who were undergoing the same process. One by one we entered the dreaded exam room.

Loaded down with blue books and sharpened pencils I took my place in the large room where for the next ten hours I attempted to demonstrate my mastery of the field. We were allowed breaks every two hours, but always monitored. Each exam was tailored-made by the candidate's committee of professors. My exam consisted of twenty-two topics from the areas of conducting, score analysis, music theory, performance practice, pedagogy, research, music history and repertoire.

"Time's up," the proctor announced and I put down my pencil. I was exhausted. After finishing the last question, my brain was fried, my hand ached and my butt was numb. The process was as grueling as I had been warned.

Wearily, I turned in a stack of bluebooks to the proctor, who looked as tired as I was, and trudged home, certain I had failed to include some vital information that would spell the ruin of my dream.

Waiting for the results, which would take about a week, was agonizing. But the time was not wasted. I was given an additional project—research a topic, write a proposal, compile a bibliography and develop a chapter outline. I was already exhausted from studying day and night for the "writtens" and filled with terror as to the results. This additional assignment overwhelmed me.

The topic I was given was so obscure I felt nausea as I read it—"The Musical Contributions of the Minnesingers." All I knew about these German poets and troubadours who roamed Europe during the Medieval ages could be put in a thimble with a lot of room left over. This project would require hours and hours of research, and I had just a few days to complete it.

Weary and exhausted, I embarked on the chore, and soon filled several shoe boxes with note cards. However, in addition to this tedious bibliographic exercise, I also had to come up with a dissertation topic. So far, I had no clue what it would be.

I had given some thought to a topic about Monteverdi, for I loved his music and performed his *Magnificent* from the *1610 Vespers* on my final conducting concert. But my fluency in Italian could best be described as *poco a poco*, and I could not bear the idea of having to master another language. For me, the required French and German were quite enough. The thought of taking more classes was unbearable.

Late one night while studying at the library, I was so exhausted I fell asleep with a book resting in my hands. As if in a dream, I sat straight up and blurted out "Hasse." I could tell by the looks on the faces around me who were deep in concentration they were annoyed by my outburst. After sheepishly apologizing for disturbing them, I thought more about what I had just uttered, while they dove back into their studies. I was sure some of them were in my exact position. They just didn't know it yet.

Yes, some aspect of Hasse would be the subject of my dissertation. The next day with renewed zeal, I dove into every source I had dug up during the preceding semesters and tried to determine how I would tackle this topic.

Since I personally knew of the two scores Dr. Novak had shown me in Vienna, both sacred works, I decided to use that knowledge as a basis. Soon the title "The Masses of Johann Adolf Hasse" formulated in my mind and I set out to fill in the gaps. As if by magic, chapter titles appeared, arranging themselves in order. Was I on to something significant? It certainly felt like it.

As with the rest of the Doctor of Musical Arts program, little did I realize what I was getting into or what lay ahead. My mantra since the first time I read the degree requirements (60 graduate 500 level or above units, two languages, four recitals, final exams and a dissertation) had always been "to just take one day at a time." I knew if I stopped to think about these hurdles, I would just give up. Instead, I did what I had to do, "one day at a time." So far it worked. Why doubt this philosophy now? Besides, what other choice did I have?

A week after taking the "writtens," the results were posted on the board outside the Music Office. Included on the list of those who passed, was my name, and it had a star next to it. I passed with honors! Grinning from ear to ear, I read the other names on the list. Not only had I passed, but so had all my colleagues, that trusty group I met during my first summer session several years ago. I let out a whoop and ran home to tell my wife the good news.

To celebrate this initial success, my colleagues and I invited our wives to join us at a local pub. We wanted to honor them for their sacrifices. They were the true heroines.

At the pub we hugged and congratulated each other, and downed our first beer in months. For most of us, it had been a long time since we allowed ourselves to relax. The preparation for the exams was arduous, and consumed every waking hour. To verify this, just ask our wives, who by now must have felt they were widowed.

We exchanged anecdotes, stories, nightmares, confessions, and then gave a collective sigh of relief. At least half of the "qualifiers" were completed. Stories circulated about our next hurdle—the "orals." We knew we would be examined by a committee of professors with whom we had done significant work, plus a representative from our "outside minor." This "minor field" had to be completely unrelated to music. In my case, I had chosen Asian Art History. Dr. Yee, a visiting professor from Harvard whom I greatly respected, would represent this exotic field on my committee. The "orals" were designed to give each professor time to question us on any topic they chose, including the results of our "writtens."

"How could I possibly prepare for such a comprehensive exam?" I blurted out as I downed another pint to numb the fear rising inside of me.

"Lots of sleep," was one of the sarcastic answers laughingly suggested by my now drunken companions. But we knew such a luxury was not a possibility due to all that loomed ahead.

With a do or die effort, I launched into the remaining assignments, spending equal time on each so as to be as prepared as I could. Often I woke from a sound sleep and tortured myself with a question I had no idea how to answer. What if they asked me this or that, was a constant tape playing in my head. My days were filled with reading books, articles, studying scores, taking notes and transcribing them into some kind of logical order so I could commit them to memory.

At last the fatal day arrived. After decades of preparation, I would have two hours to prove my worth. At the appointed time, dressed in a suit and tie, I approached the Conference Room and waited outside.

"Hey handsome, when is your oral?" one of my friends tauntingly asked.

"In about ten minutes," I answered. He almost keeled over. He was as nervous as I. Truth was, from lack of sleep and riddled with anxiety, I was numb, just hoping I could remember a few facts and the names of my professors.

Minutes later I was escorted into the room. Seated at the large table in the center were the members of my committee—the chairs of the departments of Musicology, Choral Music, Conducting, Theory and Composition, and the visiting professor of Asian Art History. The sixth chair at the head of the table was for me.

After polite introductions, the questioning began. At first, the committee was more than kind and threw me some soft-balls I handled with ease. After the first round, the questions became more probing, often based on my written exam. The third go around delved even deeper, and several times as the sweat was beading on my forehead I had to admit I did not know the answer.

Questions such as: "what is the significance of the chord clusters in measure 127 of Britten's *War Requiem* or "why didn't Bach use the same orchestration in Cantata 27 as he did in Cantata 21" left me speechless. Afraid to hazard a guess for fear of showing complete ignorance, I tried to rephrase the question, hoping to gain a little time to wrack my brain for an answer. Sometimes the tactic worked, and sometimes it backfired.

As the exam progressed, it became evident the visiting professor was impressed with my knowledge of Gregorian chant, Renaissance masses, Baroque cantatas, 19th century requiems, 20th century operas and other esoteric topics posed to me. My music professors, on the other hand, were just as impressed with my knowledge of Buddhist iconography, Ajunta Cave frescos, Ming dynasty scrolls and Chinese bronzes. But would that be enough?

Slowly and painfully the minutes ticked by. I thought I would pass out from exhaustion. My heart beating so hard, I was afraid it might burst through my chest.

Finally, the Chair halted the questioning and asked me to talk about my dissertation proposal. Hoping this was a sign I had acquitted myself with some degree of honor, I launched into my chosen topic with all the passion I could muster after two hours of being grilled. I mentioned my past history with Hasse, my personal experience with his scores, and my association with Dr. Nowak of the *Nationalbibliothek* in Vienna.

Judging from the looks on their faces, my enthusiasm was not matched by all the members of the committee. I was ill prepared for the barrage of questions hurled at me. I felt I was being personally attacked. The biggest obstacle, I was reminded, was finding music to study and analyze. In no uncertain terms would the two works I briefly saw in Vienna constitute enough material upon which to base any conclusions. The fact alone the Vienna manuscripts were copies not autographs, would question their accuracy. The majority held the opinion Hasse's music no longer existed in any form or quantity which could be considered representational.

I slumped down in my chair, feeling defeated and lost. Could I flunk my "orals" if my topic was rejected? The thought not only crossed my mind, it terrified me.

There was one exception to the majority—Dr. Hamm, the Chair of the Musicology Department. He was intrigued by my cursory findings and he believed Hasse was a significant composer, one well regarded during his long tenure.

"This topic is indeed worthy of further investigation," he instructed his esteemed colleagues. Guided by the weight of his opinion, the committee agreed to give me temporary approval, subject to review after I had conducted additional research.

Relieved yet challenged, I was escorted out of the room and told to wait in the hall while the committee deliberated. Again my life flashed before me as I agonizingly awaited the results. Had I come all this way, spent all these years, invested all this money to be told "no" or "come back in six months?" I could barely form those thoughts, so painful would rejection feel.

After what felt like hours but was just minutes, the door opened and my advisor ushered me back into the room. All were smiling as they shook my hand and congratulated me on a job well done.

There are no words to describe the relief I felt when I heard the verdict from professors I so admired and respected. Often I would recall that overwhelming feeling of relief while advising the hundreds of grad students I taught during the course of my career.

Now, one more hurdle remained. In order to be awarded a Doctor of Musical Arts, the PhD of the performing arts field, I had to write and defend a dissertation. How long this would take depended on the results of my research, my fortitude and my determination. I knew the academic world was filled with 'all buts'—persons who for one reason or another failed to complete their dissertation and who were now waiting tables or driving cabs in New York, LA, or Chicago. I was determined not to let this happen to me. I had just jumped through dozens of hoops; one more could not be so bad, plus I had the added advantage of champions in my court and enthusiasm for the topic on my side.

What next? What did I know about Hasse? Not much, just what I had read in the Grove's article and other books which gave him a cursory mention.

I had found references to Hasse as a symphonist, an opera composer, even information about his court in Dresden, but precious little on Hasse as a church composer. Had I chosen an area with countless dead ends? I knew of two major works, but were there more? If others couldn't find them how would I be more successful? As the doubts began to overcome me I thought about what to do next.

I racked my brain for clues and followed every hunch to exhaustion, but always with the same negative results. Furthermore, the sources I found were written by 19th century German scholars on topics far

16

removed from mine. True, they might reveal some biographical information, but I was hungry to find information about his church music.

With the help of my dog-eared German dictionary, the one which had seen me through the painful language exam, I began translating; quickly realizing the stilted German language, awkward construction, and formal script would be sizeable obstacles to overcome.

But my determination paid off, and soon I began to reconstruct a most fascinating life, one which revealed Hasse's importance, his contributions and his legacy. Not only was he revered during his lifetime, but so was his equally renowned wife. Faustina Bordoni, a soprano of unparalleled beauty, possessed a reputation almost the equal of her husband.

I was beginning to get a glimpse of a composer and his artist wife who had intimate contact with the musical giants of the 18th century and who were welcomed at the courts of the capitals of Europe. A fascinating story was slowly being revealed to me about this most intriguing couple.

Chapter Three: Uncharted Territory

How is it so little is known about the Hasses, the musical darlings of the eighteenth century? Why has this celebrated couple been so neglected by musicians and scholars alike—no books, no published music, and no recordings? Maybe I could unearth him. If only I could solve the puzzle—what happened to his music?

The answer, I feared, was the same everyone else came to—his music was destroyed, first by Frederick the Great and then by the Western Allies, events over which Hasse had no control. One war destroyed his palatial residence, the other his entire city.

I knew to begin my search I had to go to Dresden, the city where Hasse established his fame. But was it too risky? After all, Dresden was still recovering from WWII and lay in the very heart of communist occupied East Germany.

Having completed all course work, passed the qualifying exams, and procured a temporary approval from the committee, there was no reason for me to remain on campus. I was free to leave and begin my research. Since I had just accepted a position at the University of Arizona, and didn't have to be on campus until fall, time was on my side. If I left soon, I would have several months to make the trip.

Although I hoped my wife would go with me, she elected to return to California to see her parents and get ready for the move to Tucson, our new home. With her blessing, I set off to find the next piece of the puzzle.

I flew to Vienna, the city I fell in love with the first time I saw it in the summer of 1962, the year I finished my master's. My beloved music history teacher, Dr. Virginia Short, a woman of extraordinary gifts whom I regard as one of my mentors, invited several students to accompany her on a grand six week whirl-wind tour of Europe. This trip resembled the kind movies parodied in titles such as "If this is Tuesday it must be Belgium." I could not pass up such an invitation.

In order to see as much as we could in so short of time, we flew from city to city, raced through museums and castles, and ran to concert sites. But the doors she opened and the sights she showed me helped shape the course of my life. She encouraged me to set goals higher than I could have imagined. I saw the treasures of Europe through the eyes of one who had spent her entire life traveling and studying. I was forever changed.

I recalled hurried visits through museums, so we would not miss the most important paintings, sculptures, or art objects.

"Don't bother with this room" she would say. "The painting you must see is over here," and she would whisk us into a room displaying a Botticelli, Rembrandt or Vermeer.

She gave me the keys to the capitals of Europe—London, Paris, Rome, Florence, Venice, Vienna, Munich, as well as countless quaint villages where other treasures were found. And she gave me a thirst for knowledge, not the kind that came from books, but the kind that comes from experiences.

Her brilliant insights into the history of music, art and architecture challenged and inspired me. She encouraged me to develop my talents, to strive for the perfection she so fervently believed was imbedded within. She was my inspiration, my muse, and often during my career I would hear her wise voice guide me in just the right direction. She was like my other mother, always encouraging. She believed in my potential.

I remember the magic she wove in her music history class. She would burst into the room, loaded down with books and records, and launch into the topic of the day with such enthusiasm, the class often gave her a standing ovation after her performance, for perform she did. She didn't just lecture, she preached. She believed with all her heart that a love and passion for the arts were essential keys to finding meaning and worth in life. It was her mission to pass this philosophy on to the next generation. And we, as future teachers, were her ambassadors. We were expected to carry on the torch.

I can still picture her putting a scratchy recording of opera diva Maria Callas on an old portable phonograph, and in her trembling voice sing along, completely enveloped in the beauty of the moment. Her classes were so popular I often had to sit on the floor due to the throngs that came to watch her teach. Observing her was like watching Julia Child prepare *boeuf bourguignon*, a master at the height of her creative powers.

My trip to Europe with Dr. Short was life-changing, and as promised, I did return to Europe many times, often on concert tours, on personal adventures, or with my teen-age sons. Gazing into their young eyes as they beheld the same treasures I saw that first magical summer was worth the price of the trip. And so the torch was passed. My sons became citizens of the world, no longer limited by their southern California life style. They had a taste of other cultures, and were forever changed.

Now, I was about to embark on another European adventure, but this time with a very specific purpose—rediscover Hasse and his music. Little did I know what loomed before me, or the many hurdles I would have to conquer. But girded with enthusiasm, off I went.

ॐ   ॐ   ॐ

First stop, Vienna. After getting settled in a little *Gasthaus* in the *Viertelbezirk*, (the fourth district), reasonable lodging I read about, I spent my first evening walking the famed *Ringstrasse*. Instantly the magic returned. It was just as I left it. I wanted to pinch myself. I could not believe I was once more on the legendary tree-lined boulevard which encircled the historic inner city. In my head I could hear Dr. Short saying, "Here is the apartment where Beethoven wrote his last string quartet," or "this is the *Weinstubbe* where Schubert gathered with friends to play chamber music."

In the distance, strains of a Strauss waltz wafted from a nearby park. As I came nearer, I saw couples in elegant dress whirling about in the cool night air as the orchestra played "Tales from the Vienna Woods." Further on, the aroma of roasted espresso drifted from the *Café Sperl*, the notorious coffee house where Freud and his followers gathered to discuss theories of ego and id.

As I continued down the boulevard, I saw lines of limos inching up to the Vienna State Opera House engorging their over-dressed clientele, more eager to be seen than see.

No longer was I on a whirl-wind tour. I had time to savor, delve, and explore. I was determined to make the most of this opportunity and experience as much of this great cultural capital as I could squeeze in between the research I hoped to accomplish.

I awoke refreshed the next morning from the long flight and a good sleep and set out for the East German Consulate. Located near the *Schoenbrunn Palace*, the summer home of the Hapsburgs, the Consulate was the object of my first project—obtain a visa to Dresden.

The train took me out of the inner city and through the beautiful parks and forests once the hunting grounds for the royal Hapsburg family. After a relaxing journey, I reached my stop and began the short walk to the Consulate of the German Democratic Republic, nicknamed the "GDR."

Graceful chestnut trees lined the path offering welcome shade from the warm early morning sun. Tall stone gates proclaimed the entrance to embassy row. I approached the elegant yellow stucco mansion with confidence. Surrounded by a high barbed wire fence and guarded by GDR soldiers, the Consulate looked more like a fortress than a government office.

I took my place in the long line forming outside the entrance. Many were there, I surmised, to inquire about relatives living behind the Iron Curtain. Others, judging from the papers in their hands, were applying for visas like I was. From the looks on their forlorn faces, I guessed this day was just another futile attempt.

I, on the other hand, was full of confidence. With a letter of introduction from the curator of the Music Library in Dresden inviting me to come for an official visit, I was certain obtaining a visa from the Consulate would be a simple formality.

At the suggestion of Dr. Hamm, who had agreed to become my dissertation advisor, I had written to the Director of the Dresden State Library, Dr. Reich. I introduced myself and requested permission to search the library's music collection for Hasse manuscripts. His reply was both encouraging and discouraging.

He wrote I would be most welcome, and included a formal letter of invitation. He then added the library was still in disrepair, even after all these years since the war. He didn't know if my trip would be as fruitful as I hoped.

I wrote back, thanked him for his letter, stated I still wanted to come, and inquired if he would he be there when I planned to visit.

His next letter was more encouraging. After some searching, he had found several manuscripts I might be interested in, adding that when I knew the dates of my visit, he would make every effort to be on hand to welcome and assist me. With this news I felt much more encouraged.

After waiting in front of the Consulate for several hours, I inched my way to the head of the line. A soldier escorted me into the outer office of the Consulate, a cramped room lit by a single light bulb which cast ominous shadows on the wall, not at all what I expected to see, judging from the magnificence of the outer façade.

To the stern-looking woman sitting behind the cluttered desk, I stated my request for a visa to Dresden. I showed her my letter of introduction, trying as best I could to explain the nature of my visit.

Because my conversational German was elementary at best, her curt reply intimidated me. I couldn't understand a word. Flustered, I asked her to speak a little slower. But this made her all the more brusque and overbearing. Although I had a good reading knowledge of German, my speaking skills left much to be desired. With her thick Austrian dialect and dismissive attitude, I was faced with a formidable obstacle, the first of many I would have to surmount. Could I win her over? The prospect seemed less than hopeful.

After several more attempts, I understood what she was trying to tell me. I must fill out multiple forms and comply with the instructions and restrictions regulating visits to the GDR. None of which could be completed today, she crowed. I let out an audible sigh. She ignored me, handed me the required forms, and shooed me out the door. As I passed by the long line still waiting outside, my face was now as forlorn as theirs. So much for my first day in Vienna!

By now, it was mid afternoon. I had a lot of work to do in a very short period of time. The forms required full accounts of me, my family, as well as detailed travel plans and the names of those I would come in contact with in Dresden.

Back in my musty room, I began the arduous task of filling out the forms and reading the required material. It was not easy for an American to visit a communist country.

The hotel where foreigners stay is miles from Dresden's city center. Furthermore, all travel and hotel arrangements must be paid in advance with vouchers in US dollars. I was also required to purchase hundreds of

East German marks which are neither refundable nor valid outside the country. Other instructions stated all money taken in or out of the country must be declared; only authorized items could be purchased, and all luggage would be searched at border crossings. Reading these restrictions made me so fearful I started to question why I or anyone would want to visit such a repressive country.

Although it had been over twenty years since the war and much of West Germany had been rebuilt, the Cold War and Russian occupation had strangled the countries behind the Iron Curtain. Contact with the West was limited, and if allowed was totally controlled. I would be watched, questioned and restricted from much of the city. If I deviated from my itinerary in any way, I could be arrested for suspicion of espionage. I felt a migraine coming on.

Reading these warnings made me question if I should go on with my plans. Didn't the Consulate believe I was just a college student doing research on a composer who happened to live in Dresden? Why hadn't Hasse been the *Kapellmeister* of some other city, preferably in Austria or West Germany?

But I toiled through the night, filled out the forms, answered the questions, and planned my itinerary, all the while consulting my trusty German dictionary to make sure my answers were accurate.

I requested twelve days in Dresden and a two-day excursion to Leipzig and Halle. Although I wanted to spend as much time as possible with Dr. Reich at the Library, I also longed to see the cities of Bach and Handel as well. Foreigners are not allowed to rent cars, and flights are even more restricted, so all travel had to be by rail. I spent considerable time consulting train schedules to determine exact departure and arrival times. Based on my preliminary calculations, the trip would now cost twice what I had budgeted. But I rationalized it would be a long time, if ever, before I would make this trip again.

Chapter Four: Reflections

While filling out the forms, I thought of the last time I was in East Germany—June of 1969 on a concert tour with the Santa Clara Chorale, a choir I had founded. Our eighty-voice choir and thirty-piece orchestra, stuffed into four tour busses, had been treated royally by our hosts. We had given glorious concerts all over Europe: Baden-Baden, Berne, Lucerne, Rome, Florence, Venice, Salzburg, Vienna and Munich, and were now on our way to West Berlin for the final concert of our four-week tour by way of the East German corridor. Though excited, we were not looking forward to the arduous ride through the restricted access.

When we reached the East German border, soldiers herded us off the bus while they searched our belongings. The border was formidable, guarded by large cement barriers blocking the highway. High above in steel towers, Russian and GDR soldiers spied on our every move. I was terrified. What could they do to us? Were we naïve to include Berlin on our tour?

They collected our passports. We were shunted off to an adjacent building and allowed to use the toilets and spend some of our DDR marks at a make-shift bar. I tried to engage one of the guards in conversation, but he was in no mood.

To break the tension strangling us, I spread word around perhaps we could sing something for our "hosts." I hummed a pitch and we started, first tentatively, then as we saw the guards begin to relax, with more confidence. They loved our folk songs and spirituals. When we broke into our version of *Kalinka*, a favorite of all Russians, the room erupted and they added their lusty voices to ours. As if by magic, the atmosphere changed from abject fear to genuine camaraderie. We had won them over, and their smiles and clapping proved it. We had become one in song—what a testimony to the power of music!

Soon they returned our passports and we were allowed to re-board the bus. As the large iron gates opened, the soldiers waved goodbye and the buses inched forward into the forbidden land. We were now behind the Iron Curtain, but no longer as afraid and intimidated as we had been just moments ago. Though now "strangers in a strange land," we had seen firsthand the humanity beneath the exterior, regardless of politics and philosophy.

The bus picked up speed, and we rumbled down the deserted two-lane highway, our only link now to the Western world. Evidence of this oppressive communist state was everywhere; steel towers armed with guards surveyed the countryside; barbed wire fences cordoned off the road from the few farms and villages we passed. At major intersections, Russian tanks silently stood in menacing rows, making sure no one made unscheduled detours. Lingering near the tanks, soldiers jeered us as we rolled by. But we knew better. We had seen their softer side.

Hours later, we arrived at the West Berlin border. I could feel the tension rising in the bus. Again, huge cement bunkers blocked our way, turning the road into a series of sharp "S" turns which the bus had great difficulty maneuvering. Guards with machine guns drawn stared down from towers as we drove into "no man's area." Huge iron barriers closed behind us and bright search lights flashed on. We were trapped in their noose, which was getting tighter and tighter.

As before, our passports were taken, but this time we were told to remain on the bus while the luggage and instrument cases were off-loaded and searched. Uniformed guards shoved mirrors underneath the chassis of the bus looking for stowaways. Armed guards boarded and questioned the driver and tour guide.

We were hot and tired after the long tedious trip and anxious to get to our hotel, but were told to sit and await further instructions. A silence gripped the once raucous and cheerful riders. It was clear we would not burst into song now. Music was not going to be an international language at this border.

After waiting for more than an hour, our passports were returned, the large iron gates were lifted, and we were allowed to proceed. Passing from East Germany into West Berlin was like going from Barstow to

Vegas—neon lights flashed, the streets were brightly lit, and people and cars moved freely about. We were even greeted with a large sign: *Willkommen in Berlin*. What a welcome sight. I let out a sigh of relief, and I'm sure I wasn't alone. Although I didn't know it then, I would experience this contrast between the East and West more vividly the next day.

When we arrived at our downtown hotel, dinner was waiting. Famished and exhausted, we were treated to an elegant candle-lit roast beef dinner with all the trimmings. Never had a meal tasted so good. After the welcomed feast, most went to their rooms, but I was curious to see some of the city and invited several of the more adventurous ones to join me.

We walked for several blocks and found a beer hall. Encouraged by the raucous sounds of laughter from inside, we entered. The rustic tavern, with stag horns over the doors and folk art decorating the walls, was filled with booths and tables laden with steins of beer being hefted by Berliners of all ages. We found a table in the corner and ordered from our buxom hostess.

I was hoping to relax and unwind, but this was not to be. A man at the next table, who had heard my faltering German, came over and inquired in equally halting English, if we were Americans. Tom, the best speaker in our little group answered *jah, jah*, and the two conversed for several minutes. Soon we put our tables together and our group swelled to eight. After introductions and much prosting and clinking of glasses, we soon became engaged in one of the most fascinating yet touching conversations any of us could have imagined.

Starved about news from the "outside," our German guests peppered us with questions. Why were we in Berlin? Where would we perform? Could they attend? Was West Germany thriving? Were the US and USSR planning to go to war? Was there a spacecraft hurling its way to the moon? We answered as best we could, and with gestures and limited vocabulary, found ways to communicate.

When I asked about life in Berlin under Soviet surveillance, the friendly mood of the conversation changed. One by one our newfound acquaintances related personal stories of family and friends torn apart by the sectioning off of the city and the horror of watching the wall rise, realizing they were now living on an ever shrinking island. They were trapped.

Fritz, a ruddy faced man in his late fifties with reddish brown hair and a deep scar on his left cheek, spoke of losing his job when the Russians closed the university. No longer able to teach or conduct research, he fled to the Western sector late one night in the trunk of a friend's car, leaving his family and fiancé behind.

His original plan to emigrate to England or the US, resume his career, and work to bring his family out from behind the Iron Curtain was quickly abandoned when he received word from his mother. He learned his father had died, his brother had been sent to work in a Polish coal mine, and his fiancé, fearing he was dead, had married a GDR officer. Grief stricken, he was determined to get his mother to safety and elected to stay in Berlin and work for her release.

He joined the Resistance and planned numerous escape routes, all unsuccessful. Days turned into weeks, month, and years. Tighter and tighter the Russian's noose grew around the beleaguered city. When he saw a permanent wall being erected, complete with guard towers, mined corridors and ruthless attack dogs patrolling the perimeter, all hope for her escape vanished. He realized the city was now permanently cleaved in two, separating the free section of the West from the enslavement of the East.

Fritz spoke of brave victims killed or captured trying to escape over the wall. Some tried to tunnel under it, others to fly over it, any way they could think of to get out. Hundreds lost their lives in an attempt to gain freedom.

"See for yourself," Fritz added. "Walk by the wall near the Brandenburg Gate. It is decorated with crosses, flowers and stars, all memorials of desperate acts of courage.

The last news Fritz heard from his family was his mother had suffered a stroke and lay in a hospital somewhere outside Berlin. He never heard from her again. That was years ago. As he told us his tragic yet all too common story, tears filled his eyes and ours too.

As others at our table related similar stories, I began to understand why our visit to their war-torn city was so significant. Our coming signaled someone cared. None of us could imagine the torture and heartache of their exiled existence. To them we represented the eternal flame of hope. Our new found friends assured us our visit would be seen as a symbol of what they hoped and prayed would be their future—freedom.

After exchanging information and vowing to stay in touch, we thanked them for their warm friendship and walked back to the hotel, all the more thankful yet wiser from our serendipitous encounter.

The next day was both sobering and enlightening. After a hearty breakfast at the hotel, I boarded the bus for the city tour. We were told we would see sites in West and East Berlin, unexpected good news, for our guides had earlier warned us the border is often closed without warning.

Our bus was commanded by Brigitte, a lovely young woman in her late twenties who worked for the West Berlin Tourist Bureau. Her knowledge of the city was encyclopedic, and soon we were immersed in the history of this ancient seat of German power and culture for over a thousand years.

For several hours we drove around West Berlin, taking in the major sites. As a special perk, we were given a private tour of the newly constructed Berlin Philharmonic Hall. Located in a lush park, it shared space with the Modern Art Museum, National State Library and sculpture gardens. How I wanted to jump off the bus, run into the library and enquire if they had any manuscripts of Hasse, but time did not permit personal excursions. My schedule was full. Before this evening's concert, I had the added task of visiting the site, setting up the orchestra, and meeting with sponsors.

Next, we drove down the *Kurfürstendammstrasse*, the tree-lined boulevard some of us walked along last night. Looming ahead was the bombed-out ruins of the Berlin Cathedral. Rising out of its ashes, like a phoenix from the flames, was a tall tower and hexagonal shaped structure, both studded with blue, red and yellow glass.

Nicknamed "the lipstick and pill box" by Berliners, the *Kaiser-Willhelm Gedäkniskirche*, (Kaiser Wilhelm Memorial Church), once the site of royal weddings and coronations, was now a symbol of hope and renewal, and the religious heart of Berlin. Built out of the ruins of the old cathedral, the new cathedral was stunning. Tonight it would be the site of our concert. I could hardly believe I would be conducting in this hollowed and sacred setting.

As Brigitte told us its history, she ended by saying "it is a great honor to perform here. You can expect an overflow crowd." I started to shiver.

The next stop was the *Reichstag*, once Hitler's center of government. Situated next to the famous Brandenburg Gate where Kennedy made his famous *"Ich bin ein Berliner"* speech to the hundreds of thousands gathered in the square, the government headquarters was being rebuilt as a new, modern structure.

At the Brandenburg Gate, I had my first glimpse of the infamous wall which divided the city in two. The insurmountable barrier stood twelve feet high and was laced with barbed wire. I could see why it would be impossible to climb over. But there wasn't one wall, there were two, and they enclosed a dreaded no-man's land, a barren strip of earth more than a hundred feet wide. Impossible to navigate, the area between the walls was rumored to be peppered with land mines. Heavily guarded at major intersections by tall towers equipped with powerful search lights and armed guards, the sight of it made me shake with fear What kind of sick twisted mind could conceive of this? Something so horrific, so demonic, so permanent? Will I live long enough to see it come down?

The bus drove along the wall for several blocks until we came to Check-Point Charlie, the entrance for Westerners into East Berlin. A US soldier came aboard, welcomed us and rattled off restrictions we must follow. Once across the border, we would pick up an East German guide who would lead us on a carefully censored one-hour tour. We were not permitted to get off the bus. Pictures could only be taken at designated places. Our GDR trained guide would spout a lot of propaganda. We were to listen politely and respect her position. She was doing her job. We should take her anti-American remarks with a grain of salt. I gulped. What kind of tour is this going to be?'

The driver maneuvered the bus through the barricades to the East German check-point. Again we were boarded by a uniformed official, this time a GDR officer, who marched up and down the aisle looking for anything suspicious. Slowly, the bus drove through another set of obstacles designed to make it impossible for a run at the border with any speed.

Once inside the Russian sector, we met our guide, a plump middle-aged woman with jet black hair tied in a bun. Dressed in a pressed olive-drab uniform, she had a bright red hammer and sickle embroidered on her shirt and beret. She was aloof and detached, as if to demonstrate her superiority over us in the most graphic way. In an expressionless monotone she began her well-rehearsed spiel.

The bus crept into Brandenburg Square, but now on the opposite side of the wall. Once again, I felt the paranoia of being trapped behind the Iron Curtain as we proceeded down *Unter den Linden*, the most important boulevard in East Berlin.

The contrast between the two sectors could not have been more visible—the west side bustling with cars, trams and people, the east side eerily quiet and vacant. It was as if the people were told to hide from us.

The guide continued her speech about how East Germany was more prosperous now that it had been liberated by the Russians. She believed the real success story of the GDR had yet to be heard, and complained bitterly that the West was flooding the country with propaganda, including the preposterous rumor US astronauts were about to land on the moon. Utter nonsense she said, but we knew better. She decried Western values, claiming they fostered crime, corruption, and racial tension. She commented on civil unrest, the plight of blacks, and the working conditions of the poor. Her attacks were relentless. I could feel a sense of disgust rising up as we tried to ignore her rantings.

It was clear the real purpose of the tour was not to see the city, but rather to listen to her brainwashed speech. We drove by the massive monument dedicated to the Russian heroes of the "War of Liberation," and then past the communication tower. By far the tallest structure in East Berlin, the tower's major purpose was not to bring information to East Germans, but as we later learned, to jam radio and television signals from the West.

When I asked if we would be visiting the Pergamum Museum, one of the richest collections of ancient Persian, Greek and Roman artifacts, her swift answer was it was not on the tour. Nor was the *Staatsoper*, St. Hedwig's Cathedral nor any other cultural site, I supposed. The sole purpose of the tour, I soon realized, was to focus on Russia's contributions. No mention was made of the great pre-war cultural hub of this once proud and historic sector. Nor was there any reference to the famous authors, poets, philosophers, artists and musicians who once called the grand *Unter den Linden* their home.

Everywhere I looked was bleak and desolate. Rows and rows of post-war construction (tall austere soviet-built apartments housing hundreds of thousands of once free citizens), lined the streets. Dilapidated and graffiti covered, the buildings were decaying. Weeds crowded the streets and walkways, further evidence of the neglect pervading this sector. Where were the great parks and gardens for which Berlin was once so famous? Where were the busy outdoor cafes that used to dot this beloved boulevard once called the *Champs-Elysees* of Berlin? Gone from this side of the wall was any visible sense of civility or community now so evident in the Western sector.

Doing as we were told, we listened as the guide attempted to convince us of East Berlin's prosperity. Looking out the window, I saw no evidence of her optimism. The few people milling about were old, tired, and wearing threadbare clothes. No smiles on their faces, no evidence of joy in their hearts, just the look of years of oppression and the abandonment of hope in their eyes.

When I spotted the check point ahead, I let out a sigh of relief. At the gate, we were again boarded by GDR soldiers, and then once through the barriers, by US soldiers who welcomed us back "home." Spontaneously we burst into our National Anthem. Upon hearing us, the captain invited other soldiers onto the bus who joined in the singing. The officer thanked us for visiting Berlin, adding how much it meant to the soldiers to see American tourists. We reminded them of home, and why they were serving. We, in turn, thanked them for their service. It was no understatement to say, moved by this spontaneous exchange, that a renewed sense of patriotism swelled within us.

Filled with pride and thankfulness, we went back to the hotel where lunch awaited. Most had the rest of the day to explore. I, on the other hand, had to make sure all arrangements for concert were in order. I sensed tonight was certain to be an emotional one. We had tasted the warm hospitality of the West and witnessed firsthand the cold despair of the East, and were forever changed by the experience.

During the brief rehearsal before the concert, I placed the musicians in front of the large stone altar framed by the illuminated multi-colored glass wall. An immense bronze crucifix hovered above, with arms outstretched, welcoming all who believed. What a perfect setting for a concert that promised to be emotional and inspirational.

31

After finishing the rehearsal, the massive bronze doors opened and hundreds of people streamed in. In no time the church was full, and latecomers had to stand in the aisles. We entered to tumultuous applause, and after gracious remarks by the pastor, the concert began. I had programmed music by Brahms, Schubert, Mozart and Bach, all composers I knew our German audience would appreciate. I also included a contemporary work we had commissioned for the tour. Titled, "For the First Manned Moon Orbit," the contemporary work was set to the poem by American poet laureate James Dickey which chronicled the first time man gazed upon "that small blue marble." I felt a special reason to program the work, for on that very night astronauts from the United States were hurtling through space toward the moon.

We ended the concert with our traditional benediction, "The Lord Bless You and Keep You." Tonight it seemed to have a special meaning. The enraptured audience rose en masse and gave us a thundering ovation. Filled with pride, I stepped off the podium and gestured for the performers to join me in acknowledging the heartfelt applause.

The audience wanted more, so we sang many encores, including American folk songs and spirituals. When I indicated we had exhausted our repertoire, the pastor then came forward, invited us to hold hands, and began to pray. At the conclusion of his prayer, I recognized the words *Unser Vater*. Realizing he was closing with the Lord's Prayer, instinctively I joined in and the performers took my cue. Both in German and English, we recited together this ancient prayer that has united people of faith for almost two thousand years.

As I formed the words, tears streamed down my face. Looking around, I could see I was not alone. All sensed the emotional occasion this night had become. We had journeyed thousands of miles to this war-torn city and brought a ray of hope expressed through music. Our presence demonstrated support for Berlin's plight, and in response the audience showered us with acceptance and praise. Now we could all say, "Ich bin ein Berliner."

As we recessed out of the church to the awaiting buses, someone shouted "The Americans have landed on the moon!" Great shouts of joy rang throughout the throngs standing by. The crowd encircled us, applauding wildly, stretching out their hands and thrusting flowers into ours. The air was of complete jubilation.

A huge screen had been erected in the square in front of the church and thousands had gathered to witness this historic event. Scenes from the moon landing, including Armstrong's memorable words, "One small step for man and one giant leap for mankind," were broadcast over and over. The pastor told me another screen near the Brandenburg Gate was focused so people on the other side of the wall could see it too. I wondered if our Russian guide was watching. I knew the rest of the world was!

Chapter Five: Enlightenment

C oming back to reality in my small room in the Vienna *Gasthaus*, I finished filling out the forms and called it a day. I was exhausted by the stress and new dread I felt. Should I continue this journey, I thought, as I drifted off to sleep?

Next morning was cloudy and overcast, a good day to get a lot of errands done. With trench coat, umbrella and briefcase in hand, I first went to the bank and cashed some traveler's checks. The affable teller behind the iron bars, who reminded me of Alfred Hitchcock, was familiar with the requirements of the GDR Consulate. He assured me I could purchase the travel and housing vouchers at the American Express Office.

"You'll find it just behind the *Stephensdom* in the heart of the old city" he added. I thanked him and walked out into the cold damp air. Now, back to the Consulate.

The line in front was even longer than yesterday. I was soaking wet by the time my turn came. Presenting my completed papers to the same stern looking woman, she read them, stamped each page, gave me a receipt and told me to come back in a week for an answer. I was hoping for an earlier date, but I could tell by the scowl on her face I should not even question.

Just as I started to leave, she barked "Come back. Where is your visa to Czechoslovakia?"

"But I'm not going to Czechoslovakia, I am going to Dresden."

More shrill and angry, she bellowed because the train stopped in Prague, I must have a Czechoslovakian visa.

"Don't bother to come back here again," she harped, "until you have one." I shrugged. Another obstacle to overcome. How long would this setback take?

Feeling weary and defeated, I left the Consulate. I decided to tackle the visa hurdle later, comforting myself with the fact at least I had the rest of the day to explore. I could use the time to go visit the *Nationalbibliothek*, the library where I met Dr. Nowak and had my first glimpse of Hasse's music. That would be a great use of my time.

After introducing myself to the reference librarian, whom I was happy to see was the same one I met last time I was in Vienna, I showed her my letter of introduction from Dr. Nowak.

"Does this give me permission to use the rare book room?" I asked, almost afraid to hear her answer.

"Yes," she responded, and handed me the coveted green card which signified I was a 'scholar in residence.' "With this card, you have access to our library and others in Vienna as well."

"Including the *Gesellshaft*," I asked? For I had no idea I could get into that coveted collection.

"Yes," she again confirmed. I couldn't believe it. The *Gesellshaft der Musikfreunde* (Society of the Friends of Music) housed a wealth of masterpieces by composers such as Schumann, Liszt, Mahler, Wagner, and Schoenberg. The collection included the autograph score of the Brahms *Requiem*, a work I had conducted several times. I was awestruck by the possibility of spending time with that revered score.

As she guided me to the reading room, she added, "Dr. Nowak is out of town, but I expect him back in a few days. I am sure he will be delighted to see you when he returns." I beamed.

First, I consulted the card catalogue and made notes on references to Hasse. One book caught my attention—*Johann Adolf Hasse als Kirchenkomponist* (Hasse as Church Composer), written in 1910 by Walter Müller. Next, I located the book on the history of the Dresden Court Dr. Nowak had shown me, plus one on Hasse as a symphonist, and numerous references to articles on Hasse and his wife.

To my utter amazement, I also found nine scores attributed to Hasse, including the two works I had glimpsed during my last visit. Now, the delay for the visa seemed like a gift. I could use this extra time to study these resources, making my trip to Dresden all the more valuable.

The Müller book was a gold mine. It contained a list of manuscripts and their locations. But written prior to Europe's two devastating wars, I doubted how accurate the listings would be. Müller concluded Hasse had written at least ten masses and three requiems, copies of which could be found in libraries all over Europe, including several in Austrian monasteries not far from Vienna. How much of this music still existed was, of course, the mystery, but at least I knew where to begin my hunt.

I left the library with a smile on my face and several books in my briefcase. Time to celebrate. Feeling I had accomplished a lot in one day, I returned to my room, deposited the books on the bed, and set out for a great meal. I headed to the *Nashmarkt*, the outdoor market on the banks of the canal just blocks from the hotel.

The air was crisp and clean after the light rain and the mood festive. The market was flooded with people. Rows of shops, markets and taverns teemed with people shopping for tonight's meal or stopping for a beer before returning home. The variety of items was impressive—fruits, vegetables, meats, poultry, baked goods, desserts, cheeses, wines, flowers, and a large variety of beers were lavishly displayed. I loved being in the middle of this hubbub where few tourists ventured.

Rich aromas coming from a near-by Hungarian stall caught my attention. Soon I sat down with a stein of beer and enjoyed a delicious crock of goulash. With a gypsy fiddler playing nearby, my exotic evening was complete.

Renewed and energized, I raced back to my room and began pouring over the books. My first hurdle was reading the old German script where the "S" looks like a "G," and sentences were as long as paragraphs. But I persisted, and found information which looked promising.

Reading brief biographies of Hasse and his wife, accounts of the musical life of Dresden, and seeing excerpts of his compositions, encouraged me to continue my quest. Now I had concrete evidence that others had been interested in Hasse. So why was he still unknown?

Most fascinating, I discovered Hasse had an encounter with Bach, who was eager to leave the middle-class industrial town of Leipzig for the glamour and prestige of the Dresden court. This kernel of information intrigued me. I wanted to delve into it more. If true, it would link Hasse with the most famous musician of all time.

I found references to Hasse's wife Faustina Bordoni, a noted singer with a silvery voice. As the prima donna of her day, Hasse wrote several operas for her which proved so popular they were produced not only in Dresden, but in other European capitals as well. Faustina also sang leading roles in London with Handel's Italian Opera Company. Another interesting fact I wanted to pursue.

I read until the wee hours of the night, discovering more about this fascinating couple and their travels. After the bombardment of Dresden by Frederic the Great, the Hasse's were welcomed into the sumptuous Viennese court of the Empress Maria Theresa. There they met Haydn, the father of the symphony, the young musical prodigy Mozart, and the opera reformist Gluck. Hasse's life spanned the entire 18th century. He had personal contact with the most renowned musicians of the Baroque and Classic eras. The list of Hasse's acquaintances included Bach, Handel, Haydn, Mozart, and Gluck. What other composer could boast such a pedigree?

Although my immediate interest was in Hasse the church musician, it was apparent from my readings that he was primarily known for his operas, which were produced in the major capitals of Europe. Hasse was beginning to look like one the most famous musicians of his day, so what happened? Why do we know so little about him? Why had he been so neglected?

The next day the libraries were closed, so I decided to follow a clue mentioned in Müller's book and visit the Benedictine Abbey in *Kremsmünster*. The two-hour train ride gave me time to read and enjoy the beauty of the countryside. Earlier, I had contacted the Curate of the Abbey's library. He agreed to meet me at the train station.

"*Grüss Gott*," he shouted and waved to get my attention. The priest, dressed in the traditional Benedictine black tunic cinched at the waist with a leather belt, was not easy to miss. Short and stout and ageless in the way only priests appear to be, he was a robust man who looked like he enjoyed his meals and the famed Benedictine liqueur. Pastor von Alst had sparkling dark eyes and a toothy grin. He welcomed me and I followed him to his car in the lot behind the station.

In a blaze of dust off we went, for he was not afraid of the throttle. With his St. Christopher dangling from the rear-view mirror, he must have felt he had special protection. I, on the other hand, did not have such faith, and clung tightly to the door handle to keep from being jostled around.

He asked if I wouldn't mind if we stopped for a bite at a local tavern. While we ate, he told me about the history of the Abbey. Founded in

770 by a Bavarian Duke, the monastery had suffered horrific damage during the Napoleonic Wars and only recently had been restored to its original splendor. The library, known as a center of research and scholarship, contained important manuscript collections which had been donated to the Benedictines. He had my curiosity. What would I find here?

After lunch, we drove out of the charming village of Krems and into the countryside. From a distance, I saw the tall towers of the Abbey. The nearer we came, the more impressive the sight. The massive monastery, at least four blocks long, was crowned by an imposing church, its white-washed walls trimmed in sienna and gold, the colors of northern Austria.

I entered the massive cathedral and was transformed. Swirling white clouds and chubby cherubs hovered above. The walls were white and gold, and the church was resplendent with statues and paintings, a virtual art museum. Color and movement were everywhere, a perfect example of the Counter Reformation style which sought to reinstate the power and authority of the Catholic Church through its art and architecture.

My eye was drawn to the massive gilded altar crowned by a golden canopy, not unlike the one in St. Peter's. My first thought was what a perfect site for a concert. I imagined hearing music resonating throughout the cavernous space. After viewing the church, the priest led me down a narrow hallway to a marble staircase leading to the library.

The main reading room, though not large, was elegant. Light flooded in through tall etched windows and danced on empty study carrels. An eerie silence pervaded the vacant space. Next, we entered a smaller room lined with tall bookcases laden with thousands of documents. One shelf was labeled *Kirchenmusik*, (church music). My eyes widened.

Moments later, Father von Alst produced two tattered boxes with Hasse's name scribbled on the covers. With care, he placed them on a table and watched with anticipation as I carefully opened each one. Inside, I found two hand written manuscripts: Hasse's *Messe in F dur* and *Messe in G dur* (Mass in F major and Mass in G major). Recalling what Dr. Nowak had told me about autographs, these scores at first glance appeared to be too neat and clean to be in Hasse's hand. Like the other scores I had seen, I assumed they were copies. Nevertheless, I was excited to see them and started taking copious notes. Screwing up my courage, I asked the priest a question that had been burning inside me since the first time I laid eyes on Hasse's music.

"Is there any way that I can make a copy of these scores? They would be so valuable for my research." I knew the Illinois Library had microfilms of old manuscripts, but had no idea of how they were obtained.

"Yes, I do believe there is a way. If your university library makes a formal request, we can make a microfilm for you."

"Would I be able to keep them?"

'We don't send films to individuals. We only send them to certified institutions, like your university library. You can then check out the films from the library, depending on their policy."

More great news. I could not believe what he was telling me. Another piece of the puzzle, I thought, as I copied the reference numbers in my notebook. With microfilms in hand, I could edit the scores, write out the parts, and then perform them. My brain was spinning as I tried to process this new information. Again, little did I realize how important this discovery would become.

"Is there a form I need to fill out or fees to pay?"

"The university makes the request and pays the copying fees which depend on the number of pages. Would your university agree to do that?"

"Yes, I know they would. I have a scholarship account which will fund all of my research."

"Very good. As soon as I receive the request, I will hire a local scholar who works for the Abbey to photograph the scores. The process usually takes several weeks. You might have the films by the time you return home."

Yes, I shouted to myself. Now I could analyze, annotate and edit the scores. Surely this new information would satisfy the reservations of the dissertation committee. With this unexpected good news, I knew I was making great progress and wanted to get as much information from this knowledgeable priest as I could.

"Why do you suppose these manuscripts are here? Do you think Hasse's music was performed at the Abbey?"

"Not likely. We know much of this collection came from the Duke's own library. He probably sent one of his scribes to Dresden to make a copy of Hasse's original score."

"That's fascinating. Was that a common practice?"

"Yes," the priest replied. "Hasse, as you know, was a renowned opera composer. His works were copied and staged in courts all over Europe to satisfy royalty who wanted to see the latest theatrical sensation. His liturgical works were equally sought after."

He was confirming what I had just read. Hasse's fame was widespread. It was natural other courts would want to hear his music. That fact accounts for the many citations I found of the same work in Müller's book. If Hasse's manuscripts were housed in libraries all over Europe, could this revelation be another part of the puzzle? If I couldn't locate autographs, perhaps I could find copies of Hasse's works and compare them. This impromptu visit to the Abbey was proving to be even more valuable than I originally thought. I thanked the priest for his many kindnesses as I handed the manuscripts back to him.

Before he drove me back to the train station, we stopped for a beer at his favorite *Gasthaus* in the village. The warm hugs and handshakes he received proved how much he was loved by the townspeople. He introduced me as his new American friend and I enjoyed answering the locals many questions in my too limited German. Few tourists ventured into their village. They were curious why I was there and how I came to know their beloved priest. My brief answer about Hasse and his music seemed to satisfy their curiosity.

"Be sure to be at mass Sunday" the priest chided in jest when we left.

"*Weidersehen,*" he shouted as the train pulled away, and I echoed the same. What a wonderful day! I could not believe my good fortune. I had discovered two more works, learned about the microfilm process, and been treated with such warmth and kindness. I would find some way to thank him later, but now my thoughts were centered on returning to Vienna and getting my Czech visa.

The beauty of the countryside whizzed by and I wondered about the other monastery mentioned in Müller's book. Would I have time to make a visit there as well? But first things first. Get the visas, make the travel arrangements, and think about another trip later.

When I returned to my room, I made notes about my visit to Krems, and then began the arduous task of translating passages from the books I checked out. Working well into the night, I scratched out an outline of the first chapter—facts about Hasse's life, his travels, his compositions—all valuable information which would help me as I searched for more of his music.

The next day I had three goals: visit the Czech Consulate, contact the other monastery, and go back to the *Nationalbibliothek*. Even though deprived of sleep, I was up as soon as the sun rose.

As if Vienna was opening her arms to greet me, it was another perfect day, crystal clear, sunny and warm. How I loved being in this city with its tree-lined boulevards, magnificent churches, museums, and impressive architecture. Like Washington D.C., Vienna's sheer grandeur alone announced to the world she was a national capitol.

After a short tram ride, I was in the heart of the old city again near St. Stephen's, the main cathedral. Rounding the corner on *Brandstrasse*, I spied the American Express Office, my first stop of the day.

"*Grüss Gott*," I said to the lady seated behind the information desk. In faltering German I tried to explain my problem.

"English please," she responded, "or we will be here all day." I felt duly chastised.

"Now please tell me again, how I can help you?"

"I want to contact someone at the *Klosterneuberg*, the Monastery just outside Vienna. I'm hoping to go there and do some research."

After checking several phone books she said, "Ah, here it is. Allow me to dial it for you," and then handed me the phone. Several minutes later a man answered. Luck was on my side. He was a young priest who spoke perfect English. Although born in Linz, he had studied in Oxford, and then attended seminary in Toronto before returning to Austria, his home country. After chatting for a few minutes, he said he would be happy to meet me the next day.

"Take the *Strassenbahn* to Spitterlau and then the S 40 *Stadtbahn* to the village" he advised. "That's the easiest way to get here from Vienna. The Abbey is just a short walk from the station. When you arrive at the main office, ask for Pater Stefan. I'll come find you and give you a tour of the grounds."

"Many thanks," I blurted out, hoping he could hear the gratitude in my voice.

"*Bis Morgen*, see you tomorrow," he responded, adding that the trip would take about an hour, and I should plan to meet him at 10 o'clock.

Feeling confident I had made another valuable contact, I started to leave the office, then remembered I forgot to check for mail. One letter was waiting for me. Noticing the return address, I tore open the envelope. It was from Dr. Hamm, my advisor. I grinned as I read the good news—my Hasse topic had been given final approval, and to keep up the good work. He was impressed by my progress. What a relief. The committee had at last recognized the value of my research.

My next stop was the Czechoslovakian Consulate. Located on *Penzingerstrasse*, a beautiful tree-lined section of north Vienna, the Consulate stood next to the expansive *Augarten* where many other embassies were located.

Unlike the rude treatment I received at the GDR, the visit to the Czech office was pleasant. First, no line. Second, the information officer spoke enough English, so we easily conversed. Third, I was granted a visa on the spot, as I was only passing through the country, not making a visit. I was even able to pay the modest fee with the Austrian shillings I had in my pocket.

The whole transaction was so expedient I had several hours to kill before the library opened. I took the tram back to the city center, found a coffee house and spent the time translating notes and verifying facts from the books I checked out, knowing I might not have access to these valuable resources again.

Inside the café, the ambiance was typically Viennese. Waiters in starched white shirts, black trousers and crisp aprons rushed about with great efficiency. Echoes of Viennese waltzes filled the room from unseen speakers. Dozens of marble tables crowded the elegant room populated with locals discussing the news of the day or reading the daily paper. In spite of all the commotion, I was able to concentrate. I loved being in a space so foreign to anything I could find back home. I had to pinch myself. I was in Vienna again, a city that had so captured my heart on my first visit years ago.

After a couple of hours of diligent work, I left the café and walked through the picturesque streets of the old city to *Kärtnerstrasse*, the main shopping center. I passed Doblinger's, Vienna's legendary music store, Demel's, Austria's elegant sweet shop, and the *Michaelskirche*, the church where Haydn and Mozart often premiered their works.

After stopping for a minute to admire the magnificent interior of the church, I crossed the street to the plaza in front of the *Hofberg* and proceeded to the *Nationalbibliothek*, my second goal of the day.

When I approached the reference desk, the same kind woman told me I would find the manuscripts I requested in the Rare Book Room. I thanked her, returned the books I checked out, and opened the door to the restricted area. To my great delight, seated at his desk was Dr. Nowak.

"*Grüss Gott Herr Doktor*," I said with a warm smile on my face, so glad to see him again.

"How is your research going?" he asked as he handed me the now familiar boxes.

I told him of my progress, my trip to the monastery, and my plans to visit the *Sächishes Landesbibliothek* (Saxon State Library in Dresden) as soon as I got my visa.

"Be sure to give my regards to Dr. Reich," he added. "I haven't seen him for years, not since the Russians closed the borders. He is a fine scholar and should be a great help to you, and you to him as well."

"How is that," I countered, not being able to imagine how I could be of any help to Dr. Reich.

"The state of many libraries in East Germany, due to the war and the occupation, is such that many collections have yet to be re-catalogued. In order to save their contents from destruction, the most vulnerable libraries hid their contents in safe places. Even though it has been more than twenty years since the end of the war, the lack of funds and personnel has made it difficult to restore many libraries to their original state. As you know, Dresden suffered the most damage, by the Allies, I might add."

"Yes, I am well aware, but I still don't see how I could be of any help."

"Since you are well acquainted with 18th century music, you might be able to assist Dr. Reich identify scores still in crates and boxes." I listened carefully.

"From what I understand, forty percent of the manuscripts have yet to be reclassified, so there is much work to be done. I am certain he will appreciate any help you can give him."

Now I felt I had a mission and was even more anxious to visit this war-torn city. All that stood in my way was the visa I hoped to get sometime the next week.

"I'll leave you now to your research," he stated. "As a registered scholar, you are now allowed to have pencil and paper. You'll find the gloves on the table. Let me know when you are finished with these scores, as I have others I know you will be interested in," he muttered as he disappeared into the book stacks behind his desk, knowing full well my excitement at being able to spend time examining these priceless documents.

For the next few hours I poured over the scores. The writing was so clear I soon began to hear the music in my head, marveling at the beauty and richness of Hasse's writing. He was a forgotten genius of note, not a second rate composer worthy of anonymity. My heart pounded as I thought of the possibility of bringing his music to life. Little did I know what that thought would entail.

"I trust you are finding what you are looking for," Dr. Nowak inquired as he poked his head in the door and observed me huddled over the scores in deep concentration.

"More than I could have imagined," I responded.

"Let me know when you want to take a break, I think you will be interested to see what else I have found." With that enigmatic remark, he retreated back into his office.

Time passed quickly. Although I wanted to spend many more hours with these scores, I knew if I could obtain microfilms, of which I was now more certain, I could devote whatever time necessary to put the musical puzzle pieces together. Wanting to take full advantage of Dr. Nowak's expertise, one of the most respected scholars in his field, I rewrapped the scores, placed them in the boxes, left them on the table, and knocked on his office door.

"Come in and sit down. You'll find some interesting items on the table."

To my complete surprise, on his desk was a pile of boxes labeled *"Hasse's Kirchenmusik."* After checking my notes, I realized they were the same manuscripts listed in Müller's book—six masses and two requiems. I was stunned.

"We think these scores were once part of the Hapsburg's library. Most likely Hasse brought them to Vienna when he left Dresden to join the court of the Empress Maria Theresa. We can't confirm this, so if you intend to state what I just told you in your dissertation, be sure and footnote it, or we'll both be in trouble," he chortled as he ducked back into his office.

I used the remaining time before the library closed to make a detailed list of the works, jot down reference numbers and take some notes. If I can get microfilms of these scores, I would have more than enough material to satisfy the committee and complete the degree.

The next few days flew by. I located two more works at the *Klosterneuberg* Monastery, contacted the university research librarian, and gave her all the information needed to order the microfilms of the works I had unearthed. She was impressed at my findings, for she too had doubts as to whether I would be able to find any of Hasse's music.

On Monday, I returned to the GDR Consulate, this time with the Czech visa in hand. My visa was ready, but I was disappointed to learn it was only good for four days, not the fourteen I had requested. My application for a research visa with side trips to Leipzig and Halle had been denied. I knew by the tone of voice of my nemesis behind the desk I should not even question the decision. The look in her beady eyes told me I was lucky my request wasn't rejected altogether.

After purchasing the necessary vouchers for the train and hotel at the American Express Office, I made plans to leave for Dresden the next week. I could not believe how much I had accomplished in these last few days. As I strolled down the street toward my hotel, I listed them: (1) discovered much about Hasse and his wife; (2) located more manuscripts than I thought existed; (3) made many valuable contacts; (4) had all the papers, vouchers, tickets and visas for my journey to Dresden. Now, the real adventure was about to begin.

Chapter Six: Preparation

Packing for the trip was unnerving. Knowing everything would be searched, I thought carefully about each item before putting it in the suitcase. Should I take my Polaroid Instamatic camera? My Russian-made binoculars I bought at a flea market in Vienna? What books could I bring? There were so many questions, where to find the answers? I was not going back to the GDR Consulate again. I remember reading that I had to register with the US Embassy before traveling behind the Iron Curtain. Maybe my questions could be answered there?

"You are going where?" the woman at the information desk inquired with a note of bewilderment in her voice. The tall graceful US Embassy officer with black horn-rimmed glasses and much too much makeup glanced at my passport and directed me to a large crowded room down the hall.

"Wait here, take a number and you will be called after your passport has been checked."

I did as requested, but wondered why the hesitancy in her voice.

"Number 83, go to window 7," an invisible voice shouted thirty minutes later over a scratchy old speaker mounted on the wall in the corner.

"Do you know a trip to East Germany is considered quite dangerous now?" The officer behind the glass at window 7 chided me as I slid my papers under the slot. He had a stern look in his steel grey eyes and there was a clear warning in his voice.

"Our relations with the GDR are strained at this time," he informed me. "Several East Germans recently escaped to Austria. Security at the border has been tightened."

"Are you telling me I can't go to Dresden?" I stammered, almost afraid to hear his answer.

"No, I didn't say that," he replied, sitting up more rigid on his stool as if to assume greater authority. "We can't forbid you to go, but you need to know how dangerous your trip can become."

I gulped.

"You will be under constant surveillance and questioned everywhere you go."

As he spoke he slid open the glass window separating us, and whispered something he didn't want overheard.

"Dresden is such a desirable vacation destination for the Soviets and their families; you will see Russian soldiers everywhere. They are much more dangerous for Americans than the GDR police."

I gulped again.

"Public buildings, restaurants and hotels will be off limits to you. You must not make personal contact with anyone other than those indicated on your forms." My eyes widened.

"Limit your activities to your research at the library and plan to eat your meals at the hotel. Be on your guard at all times." Sensing my fear, he tried to calm me.

"I know how foreboding this sounds, but I urge you to take this advice. There is much suspicion on both sides now. We are telling everyone going to East Germany to exercise extreme caution."

After this stern warning his voice softened as he answered my questions. He stamped my passport and handed my papers back to me.

"Here is a pamphlet prepared by the State Department you should read. It will help you understand what to expect and how to prepare for your trip."

On my way out of the waiting room I heard him add with a satirical laugh, "Good luck, and have a safe trip. I hope we don't read about you in the papers," a reference to several Britts who were detained at the border trying to sneak something out of the country.

The pamphlet answered many questions and posed others as well. The article about the black market had the most foreboding news: foreigners must never buy anything on the street, as this is often a ploy to catch unwary tourists who soon find themselves arrested; the few stores who do sell to Westerners will be identified as *Ausländer frei*;

travelers must spend all their GDR marks before leaving the country; border guards will confiscate GDR currency they find; guards have been known to strip search; don't try to smuggle anything not declared out of the country.

The pamphlet also included the following cautionary advice: prices for tourist items are inflated and bargaining is not permitted; hotel rooms are bugged; telephone calls will be monitored; visitors are not allowed in hotel rooms; Russian agents frequent hotels where foreigners stay, so speak cautiously in public; carry identification papers with you at all times; expect to be stopped often by soldiers or police; public transportation is the safest way to travel; dress conservatively, leave valuables at home as theft in hotel rooms is common.

My head was spinning. The more I read, the more I dreaded the trip. But I had already purchased the tickets and was looking forward to meeting Dr. Reich; there was no turning back now. I had to admit I was more than apprehensive. I was frightened. Although I had traveled all over Europe, I had never been in a communist country before, at least not by myself. I can't count the trip to Berlin in 1969, as I was on a tour with guides and in East Germany for just a few hours. But I clearly remember those tension filled moments when the Russians boarded the bus and took our passports, my heart pounding and my palms sweaty.

The alarm shattered my deep sleep and I bounded out of bed onto the cold stone floor. As the sun rose, the birds outside my window sounded their clarion call, announcing the beginning of another day, but not just any day, a very special one. Today was THE day! The day I would begin my journey to Dresden.

The *Haupbahnhof*, Vienna's main train station, was teeming with travelers as I entered the massive iron doors anxiously clutching my suitcase and briefcase. Looking around, I was reminded of New York's Grand Central Station with its shiny marble floors, huge clock tower and myriads of offices, food stands, book stalls, restaurants and tunnels disappearing into the bowels of the earth. Since I already had my boarding pass, thanks to the efficient agent at the American Express, I did not have to wait in the long lines forming in front of the ticket offices.

The big board in the main waiting room listed the trains scheduled to depart for destinations all over Europe. My eyes searched the list to find mine. The trains are listed according to destination and not to departure time; it took me a few minutes before I read *"Prague, Dresden, Berlin—Gleis 7, Abfahrt 0830."* I followed the rush of people heading for the tracks, down the stairs, through the tunnel and back up the stairs and onto the platform number seven.

The site greeting me was not at all what I had expected. Was I in a refugee camp? Dozens of men, women and children dressed in tattered clothes crowded around piles of belongings, guarding their luggage, sacks of bedding, even pieces of furniture. Were they emigrating? Taking all their possessions with them to some far off country? Or were they escaping out of Hungary or Russia? I could only imagine the personal stories buried behind those anxious, even tragic faces.

The train pulled into the station at 0800 and the mad rush began. I watched with amazement as piles of possessions miraculously disappeared into the waiting cars. Since I had purchased a reserved seat, again at the suggestion of the American Express agent, I did not have to fight for a place. Each car was numbered and labeled by destination.

I found the car marked "Dresden," and hefted my luggage on board. With ease I found my seat next to a large window, stored my suitcase overhead, and used the small table in front of me to place my briefcase. Settling back in the comfortable leather seat complete with arm rests, I felt anxious, yet proud, and somewhat courageous for attempting this dangerous journey, the cautious words of the US Embassy officer echoing in my head.

At precisely 0830, the train pulled out of the station. Austrians are so efficient. Billows of steam drifted past my window as the giant engines gathered speed and whisked me out of the city and into the countryside. Looking around, there were just a few people riding with me. Were they the only ones going to Dresden? I caught a glimpse of an officer's cap in the overhead storage several rows in front of me and froze. Was I being watched already, I thought, as I crouched down in my seat so as to not be seen.

The countryside was dotted with small farm houses, barns, churches, all symbols of rural life which for centuries have anchored Austrian culture. Rolling green pastures peppered with fields of golden sunflowers and ripened corn stretched for miles in all directions. In the distance a church tower signaled the site of another small village. Farmers guided their herds through fields of tall grass. Wagons loaded with hay lumbered along twisting country roads. All is right with the world I thought, as I took in the serenity of the scene. There was no hint of the chaos I knew lay ahead, or the oppression I would sense just a few hours from this peaceful, pastoral setting.

"Fahrkarten, Reisepassen!" A shrill voice broke the momentary silence. In front of me stood a woman dressed in a grey-green uniform complete with matching beret. Her more than ample frame could barely get through the narrow aisles. After showing her my ticket and passport, she took some time perusing them. Then, her questions began. Why was I going to Dresden? Would I be stopping in Prague? How long would I be in the GDR? Did I have the proper visas? I answered as clearly as I could in my halting German, even referring several times to the traveler's phrase book I wisely had brought with me.

Apparently, something I said aroused her suspicions. I sensed a change in the conversation.

"Eine Moment," she barked, and with my passport in hand disappeared into the next car. What had I said? What had I done? I wasn't even out of Austria and already I seem to have caused some trouble. Had the dangers of my journey begun?

Several minutes later, she reappeared with another officer by her side. The tall lanky man, dressed in the same uniform but obviously her superior, approached. In halting English he questioned me.

"If you not stop in Prague, why you have Czechoslovakia visa? Where is right one?" I tried to explain I was merely following the instructions of the officer at the GDR Consulate in Vienna.

"You no need visa if not get off train in Prague," was his curt answer. "You need pass-through visa which we issue on train."

Now it was becoming clear to me. In order to continue in this car, I had to purchase a special visa from them. I surmised the money went right into their pockets, perhaps a secret source of income. After handing over 100 schillings (about $12), my passport was stamped, the original

Czech visa amended, and I settled back in my seat, thankful the problem was so easily solved.

When we reached the Czech border, I realized what the fuss was about. My car was sealed. No one was allowed to enter or leave while the train stopped for inspection. Without the necessary pass-through visa, I would have been ejected from the train. I really did avoid a crisis. Was I not clear enough when I told the officer at the Consulate that I was not stopping in Prague? Was my *"nicht"* not strong enough?

Czech soldiers boarded and proceeded down the aisle, checking tickets and passports. Noticing the voided Czech visa, the tall muscular officer with a pistol strapped to his side, questioned my papers. After explaining my situation, he stamped my passport and continued down the aisle. Crisis over. No real harm done. As I would later discover, this near altercation was just the first of many I would experience on this trip.

The officers remained on the car as the train began the next leg of the journey. Several Yugoslavians had recently escaped by slipping over the less guarded Austrian border. Extra caution was now being taken. I feared I would sense this paranoia from authorities from now on.

As the train traveled north across the border into the Czech countryside, the idyllic scenes I had just observed in Austria were now nowhere apparent. The few visible farm houses scattered over the landscape looked dilapidated, neglected. Only a handful of people worked the fields. The tractors I saw everywhere in Austria were replaced with horse-drawn plows prodded by weary-looking peasants—truly a scene similar to Millet's famous painting, "A man with a Hoe." I was reminded of the opening lines of Edwin Markham's poem inspired by the painting.

> *Bowed by the weight of centuries he leans*
> *Upon his hoe and gazes at the ground,*
> *The emptiness of ages in his face,*
> *And on his back the burdens of the world.*

His poem described the exact sight I was seeing. How did I know this classic? As a young boy I went to Edwin Markham Junior High. We had to memorize the entire poem for graduation. No where did the words seem more potent than now, as I gazed out the window at the pitiful sight.

Under communist edict, farmers were given small plots of land to cultivate, barely enough to eke out a living. Families were forced off their farms into crowded cities. Everywhere I looked, neglect was evident—overgrown pastures, malnourished livestock, crumbling barns, toppled water towers, and impassable roads.

Houses of worship, once the core of village life, were boarded up, again by edict of the Russian controlled Czech Communist Party. I sensed an air of gloom and hopelessness as we hurried past towns and villages and saw faces of this once proud nation now hollow and desperate.

Peasants, dressed in threadbare clothes carrying bundles of goods and produce, waited anxiously beside the tracks for the next local train to take them to market. They did not notice us as we sped in and out of their lives. Our sleek silver train represented a life now so far removed from their own, a life they could only dream of, a life once theirs, but now brutally taken from them.

Although gazing out the window I did not see obvious war damage in the towns and villages we passed, the true toll on these people was not the physical destruction of buildings and towns, but the emotional and spiritual destruction of their lives.

After the war, Czechoslovakia began to awaken from the nightmare of Nazi occupation. Under the enlightened leadership of President Dubček, the country was beginning to shed the oppression that had strangled her for over two decades.

On August 21, 1968, all that changed. Russian tanks rolled into Prague and crushed the hopes of those fighting for social reform. Once again, the Czech people were thrust back into totalitarian hands, but this time those hands were Russians and much more brutal. No wonder the people I saw on those train platforms looked so depressed. Three years ago, they had a taste of the freedom which had long defined their rich culture. Then, in an instant, under the weight of Russian tanks, their hopes for a freer society were crushed. Again, they were a beaten and conquered people. I saw this hopelessness deeply etched on their faces. I wondered would I see that same bleakness in Dresden. I feared I would.

During the next few hours, I curled up with a book I started reading before leaving the states. Kurt Vonnegut's fantasy, *Slaughterhouse-Five*, was an account of an American POW during the last days of WWII who witnessed the bombing of Dresden. Much of it autobiographical, I was drawn into the book by the personal stories of the horrors of war which he described in such stark detail.

On one dreaded night in 1945, over 30,000 people perished in a matter of hours. Most burned to death from the scorching heat of the inferno that erupted as the result of massive air attacks. Many, who sought shelter in the basements and tunnels that labyrinthed the city, died of suffocation. The very oxygen they breathed was sucked out of their lungs due to the fire storms raging above them. Over 90% of the historic old city, the *Aldstadt*, lay in ruins. Tens of thousands were displaced and homeless, the result of a decision to prove to Hitler that no German city was immune from the destructive power of the Allied air forces.

Known for centuries as the 'Florence of the North,' Dresden was once a beautiful cultural center situated on the peaceful River Elbe. Noted for its magnificent Italian baroque architecture, the elegant *Zwinger Palace*, the *Semper Opera House*, and its countless historic churches, some dating back to the 9th century, few thought Dresden would be targeted, especially when the war was winding down. How wrong they all were.

Tragically, most of those treasured monuments disappeared in a flash, along with tens of thousands, many who were Polish and German refugees escaping from the advancing Russian army. They sought shelter in Dresden, and the population swelled in those last few months before the end of the war from 600,000 to over a million. They too became victims of the Allies' decision to destroy the city. Not only had the bombing continued for several days, but after each initial attack, a second wave was launched several hours later, designed to disrupt the efforts of fire fighters and rescue teams who were desperately trying to extinguish the flames and tend the wounded.

I shuddered as I read more about the destruction of the city I would soon be visiting. Just what would I find when I disembarked the train— a city still in ruins? I knew much of West Germany, and West Berlin in particular, had been rebuilt as the result of the Marshall Plan, but these efforts did not include the Eastern Bloc, as Stalin rejected any such offer of help from the West.

The more I read, the more I was filled with dread. But I reminded myself I was not going to visit the city, but to meet Dr. Reich, the director of the music collection of the State Library, to examine Hasse manuscripts I hoped to unearth there.

What stories would I hear from those who lived through this nightmare? What personal accounts would Dr. Reich share with me? I was just beginning to comprehend the personal and cultural damage this once magnificent city had suffered. What else would I learn?

Years after the war, the debate continued whether this bombing was justified. Some argued it was necessary to bring about a swift end to the war and eventual surrender of the Nazi's. Others countered Dresden had no military significance and was the unfortunate target of overly ambitious generals eager to display the power and might of the Allied forces.

Still others surmised the bombing was payback for the destruction of London and the historic city of Coventry. No matter the reason, I could not imagine the horror the people of Dresden suffered. As an American, would I feel hatred from the people I met? How would I be viewed? How would I be treated?

Having lived on the West coast during the war, I remember as a young boy the prejudice and fear that spread throughout my town which was home to many Japanese families. When my playmate disappeared one night, my father said I was not to ask questions. Every family had secrets. Later, I learned about the relocation camps where thousands were forced to live in almost concentration-like conditions because they were thought of as "the enemy." Gone were their homes, their possessions, their businesses, and their dignity.

I learned firsthand the terrifying lesson: "Man's inhumanity to man knows no boundaries." There is no limit to what can be rationalized in the name of war.

I feared the destruction of Dresden was just another example. Not only had British and American forces dropped thousands of tons of bombs on this defenseless city, but they also peppered it with incendiary devices creating fire storms which consumed so many lives.

The bombings began before midnight on February 13, 1945, just months before the end of the war. The majority were asleep when the roar of planes shattered their dreams. There was no warning. When the terrified citizens fled into the streets for safety, they became entrapped in the inferno raging around them.

Vonnegut's main character, Billie Pilgrim, had one concern when he emerged from the warehouse where he was being held prisoner and ran into the streets littered with dead bodies—he did not want to burn to death.

The sights and sounds he saw became engraved in his memory —families frantically clutching to each other; mothers hurriedly wrapping their children in wet blankets to shield them from the heat; the screams of those trapped in burning buildings; the cries of children desperately searching for their siblings.

As I read this account, I could not envision such horror, and had to put the book down to regain some sense of perspective. I was afraid to imagine what I might see in a few hours when the train pulled into Dresden.

I gazed out the window. Soon, the outline of Prague appeared, its great palace and imposing cathedral etched against the azure sky. How I wished time permitted some exploration of this historic city that largely survived the ravages of the war. But that trip would have to wait until sometime later.

As the train eased into the station and came to a stop, Russian soldiers appeared out of nowhere and lined both sides of the track. Two soldiers stationed themselves at the doors of my car and again I felt isolated and claustrophobic. Huge red flags bearing the hammer and sickle hung from the smoky glass roof of the station.

Soon the "Prague" car emptied and Russian soldiers ushered the frightened passengers into the station. The once bustling platform was empty, and an eerie silence pervaded the scene. There was no doubt; we were under total submission, gripped by the heavy hand of occupation.

A smart looking middle-aged couple boarded the car and found their way to seats behind me. I was anxious to talk to them, but waited until the soldiers exited and the train began to move. From their dress and carriage, they were obviously not Czech.

"*Guten Tag*," I whispered and turned around hoping to begin a conversation.

The man answered in halting German not much better than mine. I took a chance and spoke to him in English.

"Are you going to Dresden?"

"No, we are on our way to Berlin." His answer puzzled me. What were they doing on my Dresden-bound car? He clarified the situation.

"The Berlin car is full. We were told to take seats in this one then change at the border." I understood.

"By the way, from your accent I would guess you are American. Am I correct?"

"Yes, I am from California. And you are British?"

"Spot on," he replied with a sly bit of wit in his voice. "Allow me to introduce myself. I am Dr. James Hamston and this is my wife Eileen."

Soon we were engaged in an animated conversation. I learned they were on their way to Berlin to visit friends in the British Air Force stationed there.

James, who appeared to be in his early 50's, was a tall gaunt man with a rugged complexion. From the looks of his pen-striped suit and Oxford University tie it was obvious he worked more with his mind than his hands. He told me he was a professor of nuclear physics at Merton College in Oxford and was returning from a sabbatical in Brussels where he had conducted research at NATO headquarters. Now joined by his wife, they were visiting their favorite cities, spending a week each in Paris, Vienna, Prague and Berlin.

Eileen, by contrast, was diminutive and quiet, yet possessing a most winsome smile. After several minutes, she joined the conversation. Besides raising three boys, she had a degree in veterinary medicine. The Hamstons lived on a farm just outside Oxford where she raised sheep and some cattle. James added she could raise anything she wanted as long as he didn't have to clean the stalls. He likened himself to a 'gentleman farmer' who enjoyed rural life as long as someone else did the work. My kind of man I thought.

Chatting and exchanging stories made the time pass quickly, and soon we were at the East German border. GDR officers rushed into the car and demanded tickets and passports. James and Eileen were told to grab their belongings and move quickly to the next car.

We said hurried goodbyes, exchanged addresses and vowed to stay in touch. They seemed to be fascinated by my tale of adventure, and planned to read up on Hasse as soon as they returned home.

"Let me know what you find," I called out as they disappeared down the aisle.

After they left, harassment by the guard began. Why are you going to Dresden? What do you intend to do there? Where will you be staying? Although all that information was clearly stated in the travel documents, the endless questioning made me feel uneasy. I stuttered out rehearsed answers, but not fast enough judging from the look of impatience and frustration on the officer's face.

After he tired of interrogating me, he moved on to other passengers and grilled them with equal intimidation. At least I wasn't the only one to receive the third degree.

I looked out the window and was horrified to see soldiers crawling all over the train, even under the cars. What were they looking for?

I felt a jolt as the train lurched forward and moved onto a side track. My car was uncoupled. We were left stranded there for what seemed an eternity.

Why the stall? We should have been on our way minutes after arriving at the border. Judging from the mood in the car, the other passengers too sensed something was wrong.

I heard gunshots and saw people run out of the station. Some ducked behind the train for cover. I hit the floor and lay frozen. What was going on? Angry shouts echoed, and soon GDR soldiers burst into our car and signaled everyone to remain silent. I was scared. I didn't know whether to run or hide.

I started to sit up and look around. An unseen hand slammed me back down to the floor. After the silence, I felt motion and heard rattling sounds. Our car was being coupled to another train. Engulfed in smoke, the engine churned, and in a matter of minutes we were jerked down the track and away from the station.

The gruffest officer motioned for us to get back in our seats. No explanation was given. Was someone trying to jump the border? Hitch a ride on a southern bound train? My mind was going wild thinking of the reasons for the shooting.

Not until I returned to Vienna did I learn two men disguised in GDR uniforms tried to defect. They were shot while trying to board the train bound for Vienna. One was dead and the other in critical condition. Speculation was they were aided by insiders. Little did I know then, I had been part of an international incident which sparked increased tension between the East and the West. I had every reason to be panicked and terrified.

57

Chapter Seven: Arrival

The remaining trip to Dresden was short and uneventful. Soon images I had held in my mind of this historic 'Florence of the North,' once known for her elegant Italian Baroque facades, came face to face with the reality of twenty-five years of occupation. As the train eased into the station, all I could see along the once graceful Elbe River were endless blocks of post-war construction—Russian-built apartment houses—multi-story cement coffins standing gaunt and obsolete. Already broken-down relics, they still functioned as housing for hundreds of thousands.

The train station was another reminder of the tragedy of this celebrated city. Once bustling and stylish, it was now silent, a shell of its former self. Weeds infested tile floors littered with broken glass and garbage; walls covered with angry graffiti silently screamed 'hate.' I gathered my belongings, took a deep breath and stepped off the train. More than ever, I was unsure of what lay ahead.

With my traveler's phrase book and hotel address clutched tightly in my hand, I hailed the only taxi waiting outside the deserted station. A broken-down yellow Yugo coughed and sputtered its way to me and I got in.

"Hotel zum Nussbaum, Wirthschaftweg dreizehn," I instructed the driver while trying to get comfortable in the back of the cab. The worn-out seat was covered with tape to protect me from the broken springs trying to poke through the plastic. The windows were caked with dust. Inside, the cab reeked of stale smoke. Hopeful this would be a short trip, but judging from the puzzled look on the driver's face, I sensed it wouldn't be.

His scruffy beard, long matted grey hair and pocked-marked face hinted of years of hardship he must have endured. Sensing my uneasiness, he attempted to make me feel comfortable by offering a cigarette.

"*Danke, Ich rauche nicht,*" I said, hoping he understood in my faulty German I was not a smoker. I knew my dress and speech tipped him off that I was a foreigner. He also knew from the address I gave him that I was going to the one hotel in Dresden where Westerners were allowed to stay, located miles from the city center. He refrained from asking any more questions for which I was grateful. I was still in shock, trying to recover from the events of the trip and the bleakness around me.

The taxi crawled out of the station, over the bridge and followed the Elbe as it meandered around the outskirts of the city. Soon we were in the country, the city far behind. Where is he taking me? Is this the shortest way? The longer we drove, the more apprehensive I became. The area was desolate, few houses, even fewer people. Everything looked deserted. Where was everyone?

Thirty minutes later he turned onto a dusty road and drove through a stone arch smothered in roses. In the distance I saw a large white stucco building reflecting the waning rays of the afternoon sun. Colorful flowers lined the road and large expanses of mowed fields completed the now pastoral scene. I breathed a sigh of relief. I was not being kidnapped, a thought that more than once had entered my mind. I was safely at the hotel.

The contrast between the neglect I saw in the city and this idyllic scene could not have been more striking. It was obvious this hotel was designed to make an impression on its foreign guests, its sole purpose, to proclaim East Germany's prosperity under communist control.

Checking into the hotel was easier than I thought. A very attractive young woman with long blond hair cascading over her shoulders greeted me. Dressed in crisp black and white, she appeared to be in her mid twenties. Yes, she informed me in perfect English, they had my reservation. Yes, I was prepaid, including all meals, and yes, my room was ready. I surrendered my passport, signed the registry and picked up my room key.

"Dinner is at 1900 hours. Breakfast between the hours of 7-9 and lunch from 1130-1300," she instructed me with a delightful twinkle in her eye. At first I was confused by the numbers. When she saw my puzzled look, she reminded me Europe operated on a 24 hour clock, so 1900 is seven o'clock and 1300 is one.

"The hotel doors are locked at 2230 hours," she added. "If you plan to be out later you must take your room key and show it to the night watchman to gain entrance."

Her kindness to me was evident. I was relieved to know there was someone at the hotel I could speak with.

I climbed three flights of stairs to my sparsely furnished attic room. With a slanted ceiling and a small window overlooking the back garden, it was more than adequate. I threw my suitcase on the overstuffed chair in the corner and flopped down on the much too soft bed. Exhausted from the trip and all the drama of the day, I craved a nap.

Moments later, a sharp voice coming from down the hall woke me out of a sound sleep and startled me into the realization of where I was. Is it just a loud guest or something much more nefarious? Soon there was a loud menacing knock on my door. I scrambled off the bed and frantically ran my fingers through my matted hair.

"English?" the Russian uniformed officer inquired as I opened the door a crack.

"American," I stammered. I was so frightened the words stuck in my throat.

"Travel papers?"

I ran to my briefcase and produced the documents he requested, eager to get rid of this intruder as soon as possible, my heart pounding.

"You have four days visa. You must on train to Vienna Thursday be" he stated in halting yet clear English. "Forbidden you overstay visa. I want not arrest you," he added trying to make a joke. I assured him I understood and shoved my return train ticket into his massive hand.

"Good, understand we each other?" he muttered as he handed the papers back to me and proceeded down the hallway.

I shut the door, rested my head against the wall and took a deep breath. Intimidating is hardly the word for it. The U.S. Embassy warned me I would be questioned often, but until I experienced this firsthand, I didn't realize how frightening it was. If this was a taste of what was in store for me, I'd better get my act together and appear more confident.

Now awake, I took a shower in the cramped public bathroom down the hall, changed clothes and headed downstairs for dinner. I was famished. I had not eaten since morning.

As I stepped into the dining room, I stopped to take in the scene. A massive stone fireplace adorned with trophy antlers and hunting horns dominated the room. The room looked like a mountain lodge. The walls were decorated with hand painted folk-art and large earthen pots filled with wild flowers guarded heavy oaken doors. Flower boxes laden with purple and red geraniums sat on the window sills. It was a colorful site. Long wooden tables seating six to eight were placed in neat rows. But something felt wrong with this idyllic scene. Even though brimming with guests, the room was eerily quiet.

A young boy in his teens greeted me and motioned I should find an empty chair. I was late. Most of the guests were already starting on their first course. I found a seat at a nearby table and sat down.

"Guten Abend," I muttered to the guests around me. Although nodding in acknowledgment, no one answered, their looks penetrating as they continued their hushed conversations.

There was one exception. A middle-aged couple at the end of table seemed interested in me, often glancing up from their meal to try and catch my attention. I hesitated to make eye contact. Fresh in my mind were the instructions I read before leaving Vienna, "conversations are monitored by plain clothed agents who frequent hotels and public places."

All through dinner, I could feel their eyes on me. When the other guests finished their dinner and left, the silence was broken.

"Guten Abend," the man said followed by "Good evening to you," in mannered speech that signaled he hoped I would respond in English.

After polite introductions, I learned the Sends lived in a village near-by and dine here often, as the food is the best in the region. I had to chuckle to myself, was I meeting Colonel Mustard from "Clue?" Was he going to club me in the dining room with a wrench?

Heinrich, a man I judged to be in his mid-fifties, was somewhat stout, with reddish brown slicked back hair. In his brown tweed coat, white shirt and blue tie, he was much better dressed than most of the other guests. Charlotte, his wife, was also more stylish in a light blue dress with a white lace collar. Her warm smile and bright hazel-green eyes made me feel comfortable.

Perhaps Herr and Frau Send were people I could trust. Gaining more confidence, I told them about Hasse and the purpose of my visit. Heinrich asked how long I would be in Dresden. I explained just a few days. After muttering something I didn't understand, he confessed he'd never heard of my composer.

Judging from the fact they were probably in their twenties when Dresden was bombed, I was anxious to ask them about that terrible time, but felt this was neither the time nor the place to broach the subject.

For the next fifteen minutes we exchanged pleasantries. I learned he was from Munich, had two grown daughters now living in Berlin, and was a salesman for a pharmaceutical firm. As a young man, he came to Dresden to attend technical school where he met and fell in love with a certain pretty young nurse. Charlotte blushed. He intended to return to Munich after completing his studies, but when war broke out he was forced to join the army, along with all his colleagues.

As much as I wanted to ask him about the war, I made no comments, content to let him reveal what he felt was comfortable. I told him about my family, my wife, and of growing up in northern California. Although Heinrich understood me, Charlotte's English was limited, so I tried to use my fledgling German to include her in the conversation. Heinrich often translated when he thought she did not understand.

He was anxious to share more, I could tell. It wasn't time preventing him from doing so, but his concern for who might be listening to our conversation. I noticed him constantly looking over his shoulder and around the room before speaking.

Such was my first real contact with Dresdeners, and it gave me much to think about. We said our goodbyes, hoping to see each other again. I went upstairs to my room. Tomorrow was going to be a stressful day. I needed a good night's sleep.

Chapter Eight: Research

The next morning the kind receptionist at the hotel helped me call a cab, instruct the driver, and arrange for payment. She added that he spoke a little English.

The taxi sped out of the countryside and into the outskirts of the city. I craned my head out the window to take in as much as I could. All I could see were blocks and blocks of dilapidated post-war construction. The ride back to the city was much shorter. I realized I had been 'taken for a ride' yesterday and paid much more than I should have. Another lesson learned.

"Want some of historic old city to see?" he asked in clipped yet understandable English.

I nodded "yes" and he made a sharp turn to the right. Soon the scene changed dramatically. Although piles of rubble still surrounded many of the war-damaged buildings, and bullet-pocked walls marked the scenes of hard fought battles, I also glimpsed evidence of the Baroque facades which earned this city its moniker, 'Dresden, the Florence of the North.'

We were now in the middle of the *Aldstadt*, the old city. The driver stopped in front of an ornate cluster of buildings encircling a well manicured park.

"This, the *Zwinger*, our Palace of Arts," he announced in a voice filled with pride. "Just reopened, you must visit." I agreed, but will I have time? I will be in Dresden only a few days. I wanted to spend as much time as I could in the library.

"For centuries we were great city of beauty, and then the war. Someday, someday," he muttered as he continued to drive around the park. I wasn't sure what he meant by that remark, but nodded in agreement anyway.

We crossed the river and continued north along a wide boulevard lined with shops, restaurants, department stores and hotels. Trains crammed with people whizzed past. Bikes crowded the road, and the hustle and bustle of activity was all around.

As we continued down the boulevard, the scene changed dramatically from commercial to industrial. All I could see were large non-descript warehouses with damaged walls and broken windows. Could this be where POWs were imprisoned, I thought to myself as I surveyed the desolate landscape. Why were we in this part of town?

Turning into an empty parking lot on a small side street, my kind driver announced we were here. Where, I thought? I couldn't see anything resembling a library. If it hadn't been for the large sign over the door which read *"Sächsische Landesbibliothek,"* I never would have guessed that this dilapidated building was where I was going to meet Dr. Reich.

I thanked the driver for the tour and made arrangements for him to pick me up at the end of the day. Nervously I approached the entrance and rang the bell. I had no idea what to expect.

The contrast between the magnificent library in Vienna and this cement warehouse could not have been more stark. I took a deep breath as I waited outside contemplating what I might find inside.

I knew during the war the collection had been dismantled and hidden for safekeeping, but I had no idea this important music library would still be housed in a grimy two story building that looked like it hadn't been cleaned or cared for in years. Dr. Nowak hadn't warned me of this fact. Perhaps he didn't know, for as he said, he hadn't seen Dr. Reich since before the war.

The door opened slowly. A woman in a tattered brown smock with grey hair wrapped in a well-worn scarf ushered me inside and led me to the information desk, a dingy cramped space just off the main entrance. I tried to explain to the attendant behind the desk that I had an appointment, and showed him my letter of introduction. The cold musty smell in the windowless room was less than inviting, but the greeting I received was warm and friendly. The attendant told me Dr. Reich was anxious to meet me.

He led me down a narrow hallway and rapped on a door marked *"Direktor: "Musiksammlung"* (Music Collection). A kind voice answered, *"Eintritt, bitte"* and the door opened. There stood the man I had corresponded with for months, the man who helped make this whole trip possible. Short of stature with balding grey hair, thick bifocals and a face which, though obviously having seen many tragedies, now wore a welcoming smile, he invited me into his small cluttered office.

"Guten Morgen Herr Wilson, Willkommen in Dresden."

"Guten Morgen Herr Doktor Reich," I responded and extended my hand in friendship.

After sharing a few pleasantries, for his English was much better than my German, he asked me to sit and inquired about the progress of my research. Handing him a list of scores I hoped to find in the library's collection, I told him of my success in Vienna, my work with Dr. Nowak, and my discovery of several Hasse manuscripts.

"Ah yes, Müller's citations from his book on Hasse," he said as he perused the paper. "Due to the disruption of the wars, this list is probably obsolete now." My face fell at the disappointing news.

"We are now in the process of re-cataloging our collection; the numbering system has changed. But I will see what we can do." He handed me a card catalogue drawer to begin my search.

"Where would you like me to work?" I inquired, for his office was too small for both of us.

"You may use the room next door." I smiled, relieved not be in his way.

"When you find sources you want, make a note and I will have them retrieved for you." He rubbed his hands together to ward off the cold and rewrapped a well worn scarf around his neck.

Although the weather was predicted to be mild, I took no chances and brought a sweater with me, so I was somewhat prepared for the damp and cold in his office. It was obvious from the small space heater under his desk little or no heat found its way to this part of the library. I could only imagine how cold it must be in the dead of winter.

I thanked him for his kind welcome and made myself comfortable in the nearby room. The windowless space was crowded with old wooden file cabinets, stacks of music piled on the floor, and a large table in the center of the room. I sat down, set the card catalogue in front of me, opened my briefcase, retrieved my notes, took a deep breath, and paused.

What would I find? Leafing through the cards I stopped and stared at the hand-written heading: "Hasse, Johann Adolf, 1699-1793," followed by numerous references to concertos, chamber music, operas, symphonies, oratorios, and lastly by a sub-section labeled *Kirchenmusik*.

My hands trembled as I pawed through the well-worn cards. The first card read *Messe in D dur*, 1760, Kyrie, Gloria, Sanctus, 2477/D/49 (the library call letters). My heart beat faster as card after card revealed masses and requiems attributed to Hasse, a total of eighteen references in all.

With great care I wrote down the call letters and handed the list to Dr. Reich, who was enjoying a pipe in his office, the sweet aroma filling the air, crowding out the musty smell of the building.

"I thought you would be pleased," he chortled. "These are the scores we know are Hasse's, but I am sure there are others," he said grinning as he made additional notes on my list.

"More than the ones I just found?" I inquired.

"Yes, I believe so. There are boxes of scores not yet identified and catalogued." Now, I was the one grinning.

"I am hoping you can help me identify some of these scores while you are here."

"Yes, of course, I would be honored to assist you in any way."

"You know more about Hasse's music than any of us. We will consider you our *Hasse scholar in residence*."

I floated out of the room. I had indeed made the right decision to come to Dresden, no matter the cost or danger.

Moments later he appeared with a stack of boxes in his arms. "When you have finished with these scores, I will get the others for you."

"Before I begin, may I ask you a question?" He nodded. "In Vienna, I received permission to make microfilm copies of scores I found. Is it possible to do the same with your manuscripts?"

"Normally, I would say of course, but now I am afraid it is almost impossible. I no longer have the staff to carry out such requests. But I will see what I can do," and with that less than encouraging remark, he retreated to his office.

Following him, I added, "The requests would come from my university. All costs would be paid from the graduate research fund. The microfilms would remain the property of the university library. Would that make a difference?"

"My challenge is to find someone who would photograph the scores, get permission from the authorities, and find a way to ship them." He could see the disappointment on my face.

"It is very difficult to send anything out of the country. The East German government is more protective now of her national treasures." His next statement shocked me.

"Russian soldiers have systematically looted libraries and museums, sending priceless treasures back to the U.S.S.R. We now believe the autograph of Bach's *B minor Mass* is among the stolen scores."

I reeled at the news, trying not to let him see my initial disappointment. If I wasn't able to get copies of these works, how could I study and analyze them in such a short time? I had come this far against all odds, I told myself, I am not about to give up now.

Returning to the table, I set the boxes down and opened one. I stared for several minutes at the score. Written for chorus, soloists and orchestra, the hand-written manuscript was a Mass by Hasse, dated 1780. But as I leafed through the pages, I was disappointed by what I saw. Each succeeding page became more difficult to read. The ink was washed out. Had someone spilled water on the music?

When I later inquired about the score, Dr. Reich told me the damage occurred during the war when the library contents were hidden for safekeeping in basements, warehouses or salt mines. Treasures of all kinds were preserved in this way, and unfortunately many were soiled and damaged in the process. Churches even buried stain-glass windows and sacred relics to save them from the ravages of war.

As I continued to scan the music, the manuscript became too difficult to read. This score would be of little use. It was too damaged. I crossed it off my list. However, after consulting my notes, I found there was another copy of the same work in the *Staatsbibliothek* in Berlin. Maybe all was not lost. Could this copy be another clue for me? Perhaps I was on to something I hadn't considered? If I could locate multiple copies of the same work, I would be able to compare them and identify the best copy to analyze.

I put the soiled manuscript back in its box and opened another one, *Johann Adolf Hasse, Messe in d mol, 1751*— the title inscribed in cursive on the first page. A large well-preserved manuscript, the full orchestral score was written in a clear hand. After a cursory review, I knew I had seen this music before. Checking my notes, I was right. I was holding a copy of the work Dr. Novak had shown me, the Mass written for the dedication of the *Hofkirche*, the magnificent Baroque church on the banks of the River Elbe.

Hasse's foremost patron, Augustus III, the Elector of Saxony, commissioned the construction of the church as a present for his bride, Maria Josepha, daughter of Austria's Hapsburg family. Even though Dresden lay in the heart of Lutheran Germany, the Elector built this Roman Catholic Church for his wife and her court. Hasse's Mass was written for its dedication. Nicknamed the "Wedding Cake," the elaborate silhouette of the church was often depicted by artists etched against an evening sky in views of 18th century Dresden.

I could almost sense the pomp and splendor of the service as I listened to the majestic music in my head while perusing the score. The elegant orchestral writing, the soaring melodies, the rich harmonies, it was all there, just like I remembered when I first encountered Hasse's music years earlier.

The score was a setting of the ordinary of the mass: *Kyrie*, *Gloria*, *Credo*, *Sanctus*, *Agnus Dei*, divided into many sub-movements, each with its own combination of voices and instruments. The corporate texts ("Lord have mercy" or "Glory to God") were set for full chorus and orchestra. The more personal statements ("Christ have mercy on me" or "forgive my sins") were composed for soloists and smaller instrumental ensembles. This style of dividing the text into independent movements, called a 'cantata mass,' was a common practice of Italian composers. Here was the evidence I needed to show how much the young Hasse was influenced by his sojourns to Naples and Venice. No wonder he was called *il divino Saxone*, the 'divine Saxon,' by the papal court. He had mastered the Italian style and brought it back to his native Germany.

Now, more than ever, I had to find some way to get a copy of this score. Could I just sneak it out under my coat? Of course not, but the thought did cross my mind more than once.

The next box contained the same work but in a different hand. I had several copies to make valuable comparisons. My excitement grew. I thought of the naysayers on my committee who said I wouldn't be successful. I was more than successful. I was looking at music not seen or heard for centuries. Don't tell me I can't do something, for I have a history of overcoming obstacles greater than this.

In my senior year in high school, I fell and broke my arm. It was a serious break and after the operation the doctor told me I would never have use of it. I showed him. I became a conductor! My high school counselor refused to write a recommendation for me because she said "I was not college material." I rubbed her nose in that statement by sending her my grades every semester until I graduated, and with highest honors. Maybe that's why I felt compelled to get a master's degree and now a doctorate. No, I am not a quitter.

Setting the boxes aside, I opened another: Mass in E flat major dated 1779. Next, a Mass in F major. In fact there were four copies of this mass, each in a different copyist's hand. What a goldmine, I thought, as I made critical notes of the contents of each box. I noted the forces needed to conduct the work: the number of instruments, the types of soloists, and the size of the chorus. I wrote down critical comments of each score to help me remember its contents should I not have access again.

Although there were similarities, each score showed enough individual characteristics to make it unique. I made notes of these observations and even transcribed important musical motives so I could check them later with Müller's book.

A quiet knock startled me and I stopped writing.

"Would you join me for lunch," Dr. Reich inquired as he poked his head in the door and observed me surrounded by boxes, scores and pads of paper.

"Is it time already?" As advised, I left my watch in the safe at the hotel and had lost all sense of time.

"Come next door when you are at a good stopping point," he added. "My wife packed enough food for two. There aren't any places to eat close by, and I always bring my lunch, so please be my guest."

I hadn't realized how hungry I was until I entered his office and saw the spread laid before me—a loaf of wheat bread, some cold meats, pieces of cheese, cut up fruit, and pieces of dark chocolate. What a feast I confessed as I sat down with Dr. Reich and began to share lunch with him.

69

"It is safe to talk now," he said as he broke off a piece of bread and handed it to me. "No one can overhear us in my office. I am anxious to hear news from the outside."

He said the word 'outside' like it was a foreign place. I soon realized by his many questions how isolated he felt and how censored his news was. He knew little of the threats of the "cold war" between Russia and the US, or of the success of the Marshall Plan in Western Germany, or of the efforts by our government to get Russia to tear down the Berlin wall, or even of recent US manned space missions.

He asked about Dr. Nowak, his research on Gustav Mahler's symphonies, and the state of the library in Vienna. At first I tried to downplay the success of post-war Western Europe. Convinced he was sincere, I told him there was no visible war-damage in Vienna now. All buildings, including the famed *Staatsopera*, had been restored to their original glory. Vienna once more was a thriving prosperous capital. West Berlin was also being rebuilt with the help of the Allies who daily fly in thousands of tons of food and supplies.

I told him how difficult it was for me to get a visa; I'm only allowed to remain in Dresden for a few days; I have to stay in a hotel far outside the city and eat all my meals there. I even confessed I was told not to reveal any details of my personal life, nor ask questions of anyone I should meet—just go about my business and keep to myself. As long as I remained behind the Iron Curtain, I would be watched, even followed. My room would be bugged and searched, and my calls monitored.

With each comment he gasped, often putting his hand to his mouth as if to stifle a cry. Over and over he said how sorry he was for the way I was being treated. But I reminded him if it hadn't been for his kind letter of introduction, I wouldn't have been able to make the trip at all. I was eternally grateful for his assistance.

For the remainder of our lunch together he asked about my life in the states and what I thought the future would hold. Trying to be as optimistic as possible, I shared my hope Russia and the US would find some way to coexist; Germany would be reunited; the Iron Curtain would come down, and the governments would abandon their aggressive actions which so far have led not to peace, but to the death and enslavement of millions.

With this last statement I was afraid I had gone too far, but he seemed to agree with me. His dream for his beloved Dresden was that she be returned to her rightful place, as a temple of music and the arts, free from communist control.

"Someday, someday," he muttered as he took his last sip of coffee and wiped the crumbs off his desk. Were those the same words the taxi driver used this morning? What did they mean? When I asked, he said it was a prayer of hope constantly on the lips of the people. "Someday, someday, this nightmare will be over," he repeated with emphasis.

I so wanted to ask him about the war years, the bombing of Dresden, his life now, but decided these questions should wait for another time, for I saw sadness and regret in his weary eyes.

Thanking him for sharing his lunch, I left his office and quietly closed the door. It was obvious by the contemplative look on his furrowed brow he was affected by what I had shared with him.

I returned to my work and dove in with renewed passion, examining each score, making extensive notes, observing similarities and differences, anything I could comment on when I began writing my dissertation in earnest. Before I knew it, the sun was setting and the library was about to close.

After gathering my belongings, I bade farewell to Dr. Reich, gave him a list of scores I wanted to see the next day, and thanked him for his hospitality.

"Leave everything on the table," he told me. "It will all be here for you tomorrow. *Auf Weidersehen*. See you tomorrow." He took my hand into his in a gesture of warm friendship.

"Please tell your wife how much I enjoyed her delicious lunch," I added as I closed his door.

Hoping the driver had remembered our agreed upon pick-up time, I waited outside the main door. As much as I wanted to stay and work into the night, I knew European libraries closed at 5 o'clock. Europeans were not work horses. Not like Americans.

The ride back to the hotel was uneventful, except for the fact there were Russian soldiers everywhere I looked. The trams were guarded, as were street crossings, store fronts and hotels. The city looked occupied. Why hadn't I notice them this morning?

Back at the hotel I went straight to my room and got ready for dinner. When I entered the dining room Heinrich came up and invited me to dine with him. Charlotte was at her sister's. She would not be joining us. Although at first it seemed odd he would eat here again, but I accepted his invitation anyway. We found an empty table in the corner next to the kitchen. I felt all eyes in the room turn my way and wondered how safe this meeting might be. Was I becoming too paranoid?

"How was your day at the library?" he inquired, again in perfect English. I felt he was fishing for information as I told him of my success in finding more manuscripts.

"What do you think of Dresden?" he commented out of the blue, a definite *non sequitur*.

He could not believe I had spent the entire day in the library and therefore saw nothing of the city. I could tell he was anxious to ask more probing questions, but I kept my answers short and objective. I was not about to share my conversation with Dr. Reich. The phrase "plain clothed policemen are in hotels" kept reverberating in my head as we continued talking.

My tactic was to ask him about his day, his to probe more. The conversation went on like this throughout dinner, questions back and forth with no real content. As I got up to leave, he said in a much quieter voice, "See you tomorrow night?"

I didn't know how to answer. Was he following me? What did he mean by this hushed comment? Had I said too much or given him the impression I wanted to spend more time with him? I did feel somewhat unnerved, but said "perhaps," and left the dining room.

Back in my room I spent the evening transcribing my scribbled notes, organizing them into some kind of logical fashion, and making an outline for tomorrow. As I had only a few days of productive library time, my goal was to be even more prepared now that I had an idea of what I could accomplish. The big unknown for me was whether I could get films of the manuscripts.

It felt like I was on an espionage mission, trying to break a code or smuggle out secret information from behind enemy lines. Of course Russians would be suspect if they caught an American during the height of the cold war trying to have packages sent to him. For all they knew, the films might contain secret information encoded in the musical notation. What a great plot for a best seller, I thought, as I drifted off to sleep.

I can't say it was a nightmare, but I did wake up in a cold sweat. I was being chased by a dark figure. I tried to run but my legs wouldn't move. I felt panicky. This was a new kind of dream for me. Most of my dreams were about music—standing in front of an orchestra in a large concert hall before a sold-out house. When I open the score and raise my arms to conduct I realize I've never seen the music before. Sheer panic sets in and I imagine being booed off the stage by the orchestra and audience alike. In my other reoccurring dream I am in the wings about to go on stage, but instead of being dressed in white tie and tails like everyone else, I am still in jeans and a T-shirt.

My sister-in-law, an actress who lives in London, told me her nightmare dream. She is shoved on-stage in a play she has never read and expected to carry the lead, and of course there is a big movie producer in the audience.

Funny, how in dreams, we find ourselves in such awkward situations. But this latest dream of being chased and not able to move seemed all too real. Could it have something to do with the dinner conversation? Was I becoming so paranoid being behind the Iron Curtain that my fears invaded my sleep? I rolled over and tried to think of more pleasant things.

Chapter Nine: Revelations

The next morning, I was back at the library. Dr. Reich was more than cheerful as he handed me another stack of boxes. "Can you save time for me this morning? I need your help identifying some scores."

"Of course, gladly," I answered, so proud to think there was some way I could repay his many kindnesses.

I spread my notes on the table, opened the box on top of the stack and unwrapped the protected contents. The title page read *Messe in F dur*, another impressive setting of the mass for chorus, soloists and orchestra. I noticed similarities between this score and others I had seen: Hasse's use of instruments, number of movements, division of the text between the chorus and soloists, and the overall structure. A definite pattern seemed to be emerging.

Did Hasse's other works fit this same formula? Was I beginning to unravel the mystery of his compositional style? Could I recognize his work just by looking at it? Hearing it in my head? That was my goal. I wanted to so saturate myself in his music I could convincingly describe his style, a big order in so short a time.

After checking my notes, I realized the Vienna library also had a copy of this mass. Not a coincidence I thought. The fact other libraries had duplicates of Hasse's manuscripts was proof enough for me that he was a major musical figure in his day. He didn't deserve the second-rate reputation just because no one bothered to hunt down his music. For a composer whose works were said to be destroyed, who was all but written off by music historians, I was gathering evidence to the contrary

Another rap on the door. Was it lunch time already?

"Is this a good time for you to stop your work and come with me?" Dr. Reich asked. "I need you to help me solve some riddles."

"Yes, of course. Besides I need to take a break, move around and get my blood circulating. I've been riveted to this chair far too long."

I followed him upstairs to a much larger windowless room with boxes stacked on the floor. A single light bulb hung from the ceiling, casting ominous shadows on the walls. I had an eerie feeling some POW may have been tortured here. Cautiously I settled in a chair and tried not to think about the screams this room might have heard.

"Here is music we can't identify but think may be Hasse's," he added as he handed me a crumpled stack of hand written pages. "Please take a look and let me know what you think."

I studied the pages in front of me and soon recognized the source.

"This is his Mass in F. I am sure of it," I blurted out. "There are two other copies downstairs on the table, and I know of one other in Vienna."

Obviously delighted by my observation, Dr. Reich filled out a form with the information, placed it on the manuscript and handed me another stack of papers.

This time the task was harder. It took me some time before several things jumped out at me. First, was the use of clarinets, an instrument not championed until much later by Mozart. In fact, one of the last compositions Mozart finished before his premature death was a concerto for clarinet and orchestra. It was written for his dear friend Anton Stadler in 1791. As a clarinet major, I often played it at competitions and on recitals in high school and college.

The other unusual feature was the lack of figured bass, the numbers found beneath the bass line indicating the harmonic progression of the piece. No, this was not Hasse. It looked like a much later work, perhaps by Cherubini or an unknown contemporary of Beethoven. Dr. Reich agreed and set the pages aside.

The next score was visibly damaged. The edges of the pages had turned brown and were starting to crumble. I exercised extreme care as I leafed through the work. The text was from a requiem mass and the music looked somewhat familiar. But it wasn't until I saw the opening of the 'Dies Irae,' the text about the Last Judgment, did it dawn on me. There was no mistaking the opening rhythmic motive in the violins.

With some certainty I told Dr. Reich the score was Hasse's *C major Requiem*, written in 1763 for the funeral of his great patron Augustus III, King of Poland and Elector of Saxony. Even though Hasse and his wife had by then moved to Vienna to join the court of the Empress Maria Theresa, he felt obliged to write the funeral music for his dear friend and generous benefactor. Dr. Reich was impressed by my comments, and I felt our friendship and respect for each other grow stronger.

For the next several hours I examined score after score, judging some to be authentic and some by other composers. I felt like an art dealer at Christies, authenticating masterpieces which were to go on the auction block the next week. I was humbled by the confidence Dr. Reich placed in me, and by his faith in my ability to identify these heretofore un-catalogued works.

What astonished me was the sheer number of crates and boxes scattered about the room. Caked with dust it looked like they had recently been dug out of the ground. If the condition of these boxes was any indication of the lack of interest and funding by Russian and East German governments, what hope did I have Dr. Reich would find the resources to film the scores I so desperately needed for my research.

I was jolted out of the blue when Dr. Reich inquired, "If I could have your visa extended, would you be able to stay until the end of the week? You have no idea how valuable your help has been to me."

"Why yes, of course," I responded, too quickly to know what I was agreeing to. "Do you think it's possible? I tried to get a longer visa, but the request was denied. I was even made to feel lucky to have gotten a visa at all."

"I'll make some calls and let you know as soon as I get an answer." Handing me a small basket with a red and white checkered cloth draped over it he added, "Here is a little lunch Frau Reich prepared just for you."

He disappeared and I resumed sifting through the mounds of papers surrounding me. Some of the works I recognized and set them aside. Others just didn't fit the formula I now believed to characterize Hasse's style.

I found a curious looking score in the key of E flat, but the title page was missing. It appeared to be a mass setting, as I could make out the word "Kyrie" under one of the vocal lines. By carefully leafing through the fragile pages it had every appearance of a Hasse work. The more I examined it, the more convinced I became.

Stopping to have a bite to eat, I looked around the room. There were boxes labeled Schütz, Hassler, Quantz and Telemann. I was excited to think if I opened them I might find original manuscripts by these 17th and 18th century masters. I was tempted, but dared not disturb anything for fear of getting caught snooping.

Just then, Dr. Reich came bounding into the room. "It took me some doing," he said with a sense of great accomplishment, "but I managed to have your visa extended until the end of the week. Your hotel and train reservations will be changed. The library will pay the additional cost of your stay, giving you an additional three days. Is that all right for you?"

"Of course it is. How can I ever thank you," I stammered, completely overcome by this sudden change of events. I started to feel chocked up. What an extraordinary act of generosity. My visa has been extended. I can stay for three more days. He had probably spoken to someone high up in the Consulate and told him I was of value and needed more time to complete a project. This request set wheels in motion. Word was given to an underling who was instructed to make the necessary arrangements, including hotel and train travel. It was all very efficient, German efficient. I was dumfounded to think I had made such an impression on Dr. Reich.

"I insist on reimbursing you," I added, but he would hear nothing of it.

So after many *dankes* we got back to work. For the remainder of the day, I sifted through stacks of manuscripts and sorted them into piles labeled "known composers," "probable composers," and "unknown." My job was to concentrate on vocal works (operas, cantatas, oratorios, masses, motets and requiems), whereas Dr. Reich focused on instrumental and secular works like symphonies, concertos, and chamber music. As a result of this fine sifting, I located several works other than masses and requiems with Hasse's imprint on them, including an oratorio, and dozens of motets.

The most important new work I found was a *Te Deum*, dated 1751. Marked for the dedication of the *Hofkirche*, it was a companion piece to the mass written for the same occasion. A multi-movement work for chorus, soloists and orchestra, the *Te Deum* served as a great hymn of praise to accompany the grand liturgical procession. This companion piece would prove invaluable. I added it to the list of requested microfilms.

Next, with Dr. Reich's and several assistants' help, we moved the boxes and crates, arranging them according to genre and composer. The room took on a whole new look. We were making progress.

All too soon, I heard a whistle in the distance signaling five o'clock, time for the library to close. Dr. Reich walked me to the front door and bade me farewell.

"*Bis Morgen*," he exclaimed as I sauntered down the street. Today, my plan was bolder. I wanted to take the streetcar through the city to the train station, where I would grab a cab back to the hotel, this time telling the driver how to get there. I was not going to be taken for another ride.

In a matter of minutes, the tram arrived, and I climbed on board. Soon, I became entangled in a sea of people pushing and shoving, all trying to find room in the crowded car. I hoped to find a place near the window, so I could see some of the city, but this proved impossible due to the people pressed against me. As I settled in, it was not the crowded conditions I noticed, but the absolute silence. No one said a word or made eye contact. Heads remained bowed. Was I on a train of blind, deaf, mutes?

The silence was broken when the conductor shouted "*Central Albertplatz*" over the din of the train as it made its way along the tracks imbedded in the cobblestone streets. Why not get off here, I thought, and walk the rest of the way to the station just across the river. I would see a lot more of the city on foot.

I had little choice, for when the train came to a full stop I was pushed out and onto the street. Although no one seemed to pay obvious attention, I felt their eyes nevertheless as I fought to get my bearings.

For the first time since I arrived, I had time to assess close at hand the damage caused by the war. Piles of stones lined the streets where once elegant buildings proudly stood. Evidence of neglect was everywhere. Weeds struggled to grow in cracks in the sidewalks, and boarded-up windows attempted to hide the destruction inside.

Most people flocked to the small market stands surrounding the huge square. I followed the crowd and observed. Although produce seemed to be plentiful, high-prices and inflation kept many from purchasing anything other than bare essentials. My eyes followed a group of women sorting through a basket of onions as if looking for a lost pearl. Their

78

sunken eyes, hunched-over bodies, and worn-out clothes spoke volumes as to the hardships they have endured.

Haunted by this vision, I continued down the main street, once an elegant neighborhood of private homes, and now crammed with post-war apartment towers. The people around me walked fast and so did I. No one wanted to attract the attention of Russian soldiers guarding every intersection.

Crossing over the Elbe River on the *Augustusbrücke*, I came to the heart of the old city. The scene immediately changed. The streets were cleared of rubble. There was evidence of rebuilding all around. Huge cranes lifted massive steel beams. The hum of jackhammers and bulldozers permeated the air. Scaffolding climbed up half-completed buildings and hard-hats rushed around with tools and plans in their hands. I was in the heart of a massive effort to restore Dresden to its original glory.

When first proposed, the reconstruction plan was rejected by the occupying communists. They wanted to rebuild Dresden as a monument to the heroism of the Russians, who they believed "liberated" the city from the death-grip of the Nazi regime. But the people, backed by the local government, forced the Russians to abandon their plans. The restoration of historic Dresden was seen by its citizens as a symbol of civic pride.

Crossing the street, I came face to face with the bombed out ruins of the church I had read so much about—the *Hofkirche*, the royal Catholic Church, Hasse's church. The result of a direct hit during the "night of terror" by the Allies, the roof had collapsed and fire had gutted the interior.

I tried to reconstruct its original splendor and hear Hasse's music in my head, but I could not crowd out the overwhelming feeling I had standing in the midst of the rubble—man's inhumanity to man simply knows no bounds. Why? Why I kept asking myself, in one blinding night the loss of so many innocent and the destruction of so much that was beautiful. It all seemed so senseless to me. And to think my government was responsible, made it even more painful.

Continuing on, the scene changed again. I came to a magnificent arcade of symmetrical pavilions enclosing a large garden courtyard, the same site the taxi driver had shown me this morning. Nicknamed the

Zwinger, meaning "outward," it was so named because its canons were originally placed between the inner and outer walls. I remember he called it the "Palace of the Arts." As I stood there and had a chance to take it all in, I agreed with him, it was indeed a "palace." Rebuilt in the ornate style of the early 1700s, Augustus the Strong dedicated this edifice to his queen.

I imaged the splendor of gilded coaches drawn by proudly festooned teams of horses encircling the courtyard, stopping to deposit their overdressed and bejeweled patrons for a gala evening. So ornate were the buildings, the best example of the late Baroque style molded into stone I had ever seen, that for a moment I forgot I was in a war-torn city. The graceful rows of windows decorated with flowered filigree; Greek and Roman mythology artfully carved into immense pillars surrounded the massive doorways; gilded cupolas and crowned gates; colorfully designed gardens and majestic fountains, all attested to an age of opulence which rivaled any court in Europe. It was Augustus the Strong's *Versailles*, a testament to his wealth and power. For thirty years Hasse served as music director for this royal family and produced many musical spectacles here. Could I even imagine what he might have witnessed?

How did this building survive in the midst of so much destruction? Well, in fact I soon learned it didn't. The plaque planted in front of the main gate told something of its history. The Palace, along with most of Dresden, was indeed destroyed on those February nights in 1945 during the carpet-bombing raids.

Against severe pressure from the Soviets, the people of Dresden voted to rebuild the *Zwinger* Palace, and it became the first building restored after the war ended. Rather than have the ruins razed and replaced by a monument to Russian glory, the citizens rallied to save some shred of their glorious past. Hopefully, now that I am able to stay a few days longer, I will find time to visit the museums and art galleries inside.

Continuing toward the train station, again I was shocked, not by beauty, but by the ugliness of what I saw—gaping holes in the ground where bombs landed, acres of twisted steel and broken stone, and walls riddled by bullets. Why? Why?

Brushing these dark thoughts aside, I continued. The streets were quiet now. Most of the people had returned to their small apartments in the huge multi-storied complexes. A train whistle and the sight of smoke rising in the cool air signaled I was close to my destination.

Although glad I didn't take a cab home from the library, I was saddened by the sights I had just seen. So much destruction. The one glimmer of hope was the reconstruction of the *Zwinger*. No wonder the people of Dresden fought to restore this important symbol of their gloried past before addressing the other needs of the city. The *Zwinger* was a symbol of Dresden's rich and storied heritage and a glimpse of what she could once more become.

Back at the hotel, I was not hungry, but decided to make an appearance in the dining room just in case my absence might be construed as suspect. I found an empty seat, ordered a beer, and tried to reconstruct the events of the day. What a day it was—manuscripts discovered, visa extended, city sights seen—my head was spinning.

I was jolted back to reality when I felt a hand on my shoulder.

"You must come join us," a voice said. "We have been looking for you. Please come."

Turning around I recognized Heinrich who beckoned me.

"Thank you," I rather unenthusiastically replied, for all I wanted to do was have a quick bite and return to my room so I could organize my notes and do some reading.

However, joining the Sends proved to be a gift, for I was able to ask him about many of the sights I had seen today. He agreed the *Zwinger* was a symbol for the people of Dresden, and he hoped the entire city would someday be restored to its former glory. How confident was he this would happen soon? Not at all, he told me in hushed tones, for the Soviets were still taking money and resources out of the country to rebuild war-torn Russia. The reason Dresden was receiving any attention at all was the fact she had become a desired tourist destination for Russian diplomats and their families, a stopping off place on their way to the Yugoslavian coast.

Gaining more confidence, I lowered my guard and relayed to Heinrich the events of my day, including the fact I would be staying a few extra days to help Dr. Reich complete some projects. His face lit up. He turned to whisper something to his wife who appeared to nod in agreement.

I tried to figure out what it was that made them react, but soon I was lost in a barrage of questions about my work, the library, the music and Dr. Reich. I sensed they wanted to ask more personal questions, as did I, but refrained because of the danger of revealing too much in a public place. Heinrich did add, as I rose to excuse myself, he hoped there might be an opportunity to talk at length. Just what he meant by that remark I couldn't tell. I decided not to explore it, at least not now.

I thanked them for their company and retired to my room. Dark shadows from the full moon filtered through the tree branches and danced on the wall as I lay on top of the bed and took a deep breath. Was I getting too personal? Did I reveal something I shouldn't have? A thousand thoughts swirled around my head, but exhausted from the day, the trip, the tension, the task, I just wanted to close my eyes for a short nap.

The loud ring of the phone jolted me out of sleep. "Herr Wilson," a charming voice inquired, "Please come to the main desk as soon as you can."

Panicking, I splashed some water on my face and raced down the stairs, my heart pounding. At the bottom of the staircase I slowed down, trying to act as if there was nothing wrong, even though I could feel the adrenalin race through my body. What had I done? Why the urgency?

As I entered the lobby, I expected to see a Russian soldier. Instead, I was pleasantly surprised. The same lovely young woman who greeted me, when I first arrived, was smiling from behind the registration desk.

"We just received a cable from Dr. Reich stating you would be staying at the hotel until Saturday as a guest of the State Library. I just need to confirm your plans so I can change your reservation."

Much relieved by this news, I told her the information was correct. Dr. Reich would give me new travel documents when I next saw him.

"You must be a very important person," she said with a slight twinkle in her eye. "A change in visa status is rare."

"Just helping with a library project that is taking a little longer to complete than originally planned," I answered, trying not to arouse any suspicion, for I still felt waves of paranoia whenever I interfaced with an official, even a lovely desk clerk.

Back in my room, I locked the door and leaned against the wall. Why the urgency? Couldn't she have waited until the next day to

82

confirm my reservations? Is someone suspicious of what I was doing and why I was here? Again my head filled with thoughts of doubts and I felt a pounding headache coming on. Should I tell Dr. Reich it is just too dangerous for me to stay? Did he manage to convince the authorities to give me a few more days? What about my train reservation? Could he have changed that too as he said? As if this journey wasn't difficult enough, now it seemed mired in "what ifs."

After taking a deep breath, I decided to trust Dr. Reich and be grateful for the extra days. Maybe I could book a later train on Saturday so I would have the bulk of the day to explore. That would be an added plus.

I tried to tackle the job of transcribing my notes from the day's findings, but soon my head was on the table. I could no longer keep my eyes open. Too much excitement for one day.

Chapter Ten: Jubilation

The next morning at the library proved to be even more productive. Together with Dr. Reich, I sorted and labeled boxes of scores, identified more Hasse manuscripts, and enjoyed another delicious lunch provided by Mrs. Reich. I sensed a feeling of openness with the staff. As their trust in me grew, they cautiously asked questions about my research, my trip and my personal life.

During a break in the afternoon, I detected a subtle change of mood in Dr. Reich. He seemed more pensive as he quietly invited me into his office and locked the door.

"Tomorrow will be your last day with us, and it will no doubt be somewhat hectic. I wanted to take a moment to thank you for coming, for helping us, and to ask you some questions. Do you mind?"

"Not at all," I replied, for there was much I wanted to ask him as well.

For the next hour we peppered each other with questions, some very personal. He wanted to know about my family, my education, my thoughts about the Cold War, my impressions of East Germany in general and Dresden in particular. I wanted to know about his life behind the Iron Curtain. How did he survive the destruction of the city? Did he feel safe here now? Was he in any personal danger by helping me?

He told me he received his doctorate in musicology from the University of Berlin. In 1938 he moved to Dresden to become the director of the Music Department at the State Library, a highly coveted position. His two sons stayed in Berlin to finish their schooling. Once finished, they were drafted into Hitler's army. One was killed during the invasion of Italy, and the other, soon after the death of his younger brother, fled to Sweden. The last time he heard from his son was several years ago. The news both cheered and saddened him. He learned his son had married, had three children, and was now living in a village outside of Gothenburg.

Although he tried many times to contact his son, his letters came back unanswered, some even opened and censored. Tears welled up as he told his story. His greatest wish before he died was to see his son and grandchildren. I choked up too, thinking about what it must be like to be separated from your family, and there was not a thing you could do about it.

I pressed him for more information about life in Dresden. At first he was reluctant. He did say because he lived out in the country he was able to escape the bombing, but many of his friends and co-workers were not so fortunate. If they only had some warning, he said over and over again.

"Life under the Russians was unbearable," he told me as he started to open up more. "But now that the East German government is gaining more power, things are getting better. Food and durable goods are more abundant. The economy is beginning to recover from run-away inflation, and we no longer have to rely upon the Black Market."

"Do you have any hope for a unified Germany?"

"At first I did, but not anymore. Hoping is too painful," he added, as tears began to form. "It has been over twenty years since the Russians invaded. Now we just exist and persevere. I doubt I will see any real change in my lifetime."

Again I asked about the microfilms. "Make a list of the scores you want and I will see what I can do," he wearily answered. Not wanting to press the issue, I hoped he might have a plan but was reluctant to tell me in case it didn't work out. I had to trust him, and of course I did. He knew how valuable the films would be to my research, yet we both knew of the danger of trying to send documents to a foreign country, especially the US. All packages and mail were inspected and censored. He would have to be careful not to endanger his position or his staff. I knew this too, so for the time being I let the matter go.

At the end of the day I thanked him for his hospitality and friendship and took a cab back to the hotel. After dinner, this time thankfully by myself, I spent the entire evening recopying my notes, making a list of the manuscripts I wanted filmed, and writing in my journal so I could share these extraordinary days with my wife when I returned home. In

Vienna I wrote almost daily, but I was afraid to send her anything out of East Germany.

When I first started traveling, on that magical trip with Dr. Short, I formed the habit of capturing my thoughts and impressions on paper each night before I went to sleep, while they were still fresh in my mind. I have done this on every trip since. While detailing today's events in my journal, I vowed someday to write a book about my adventures, especially this one, which was turning out to be more fruitful than I could have imagined.

❧   ❧   ❧

My last day at the library was hectic but also sad. I had grown so fond of Dr. Reich and his staff. It hurt to know I would soon be saying goodbye and returning to another world, a world they could only imagine.

The morning was busy with the usual tasks of sorting and identifying. Then around noon, one by one the staff left. The room was empty except for me. I wondered if something had happened, or if an unannounced important visitor had just arrived. In the absence of an explanation, I continued with my work.

Several minutes later, I heard a loud voice say "Herr Wilson, please come downstairs, we need you for a minute."

Thinking it was just another score they wanted me to examine, I went downstairs in the direction of the booming voice. I entered a large room at the end of the hall and was stunned. Hanging from the walls were large hand-painted signs: *Danke, Bon Voyage* and *Weidersehen*. The staff had gathered to give me a surprise going-away party.

Speechless, I stood in the middle of the room and gazed around at the faces of my newly made friends. I recalled how stern and distant they seemed when I first met them. Now they were warm and friendly, as if I had known them for years. What a difference a few days make. I was no longer the enemy. They were no longer spies.

The staff was assembled around a table in the center of the room laden with food lovingly prepared for the occasion—a veritable feast.

In my best German I tried to express my thanks, but my words were drowned out by their cheers. I was crucifying their language and they loved it. A tall lanky man, who did most of the heavy lifting of the crates and boxes, imitated me, which brought gales of laughter.

After enjoying lunch, Dr. Reich asked me to step forward. The room became quiet. I felt somewhat embarrassed.

"I have something for you which I hope will help in your research and remind you of your first trip to Dresden." His voice was warm and compassionate.

The room buzzed with anticipation as he handed me a package tied with bright red, white and blue ribbons.

Nervously I untied it and unfolded the paper. I could not believe my eyes. My new friends sensed how special this gift was and began to applaud. Dr. Reich had given me a facsimile of the book Dr. Nowak showed me in Vienna.

Titled *Zur Geshichte der Musik und des Theaters am Hofe zu Dresden* (The History of Music and Theater at the Court in Dresden), the book was written in 1861 by the noted German historian Maritz Fürstenau. It chronicled Hasse's years at the Dresden court and would be an invaluable source of anecdotes about his life and music.

"How can I ever thank you? " I stammered, trying to express how priceless this book was to me. I had planned to spend time with Dr. Nowak's copy when I returned to Vienna, but now I had one of my own. I would be able to translate the entire book for my research. Instinctively I hugged Dr. Reich. How could I ever repay him for all he had done for me, let alone for this precious gift? I will find a way, I thought, as soon as I get home.

After more feasting and celebrating, we returned to work, for there was much to be done before the sun set, this time the last for me. The upstairs room hummed with activity. We arranged boxes of uncatalogued music according to era and genre, filled out cards with pertinent information, affixed labels to files containing descriptions of the contents of each box, and made lists of all we had accomplished over the last few days.

How I longed to stay and see this gigantic project to completion. The goal was to re-catalogue every identified work, repair and rebind the damaged ones, and then place them on the shelves so scholars would at last have access. Knowing I helped make a dent in the project, I was proud to have played a part.

But now it was time to go back home and begin my own research. I was so grateful for this opportunity to discover many priceless scores and meet so many kind and dedicated people. Saying goodbye for the last time was painful. Dr. Reich silently hugged me as I left his office. There were no words left to say. We had said them all. My only hope was if someday I returned he would still be here.

Back at the hotel the desk clerk handed me my visa and train ticket. I was delighted to see I was booked on the 4:30 express due to arrive in Vienna around ten o'clock. Just as I hoped, the later departure would give me ample time to explore the city.

I raced upstairs clutching the new papers in my hand and plopped down on the bed. After the wonderful feast I enjoyed with the library staff, I was not hungry. Yet I still felt obligated to show up in the dining room and be counted. Even though I had felt such freedom with Dr. Reich and his colleagues, I again reminded myself I was still behind the Iron Curtain and must be on my guard at all times. Even Dr. Reich advised me of the same.

No sooner had I sat down at a vacant table, when Heinrich and his wife approached and asked me to join them. They seemed particularly excited to see me. I followed them to their table in the corner, this time farthest from the kitchen. Did they eat dinner here that often, or were they trying to make some kind of contact?

I wiped away any suspicious thoughts and decided to simply enjoy their company. Today, I had been shown how gracious my Dresden colleagues were to me. Tonight could be just another example of such hospitality.

No longer an oddity, I felt more comfortable. Few people in the room appeared to pay any attention to me. As soon as soup was served, the questions began. When was I leaving? Where else was I going? How long would I be in Europe? When would I be back in the States? I hardly had time to put a spoonful in my mouth before the next the volley came.

Right in the middle of the questioning Heinrich leaned over and whispered, "Do you have plans for this evening?"

Catching me off guard I said, "No, nothing special, just packing and getting ready to leave."

"Then you must come with us to our home," he said with great enthusiasm, his wife nodding in agreement.

"I can't, I'm not allowed," I stammered, not able to believe what I had just heard.

"Of course you are. We have a plan." He leaned closer so he could whisper something in my ear. "After dinner, meet us in the parking lot behind the hotel. No one will see you there."

"Is it safe? What about the police or Russian soldiers? What if they catch me sneaking out?"

"You don't have anything to worry about. They tell all guests to be wary. But people come here precisely because they have more freedom, far from the prying eyes you feel everywhere in the city."

"I'm not sure I should risk it."

"I assure you, there is nothing to worry about. You will be perfectly safe." There was an added assurance in his voice.

"But what about the night watchman?"

"We will bring you back to the hotel before closing so you won't have to ring for him. Just remember to bring your room key."

Although my first reaction was "NO, this is too dangerous," I was curious to have a candid conversation with people who had lived through so much. Against my better judgment I said yes, I would be honored to be a guest in their home.

Just as planned, I went to my room, grabbed my coat and a package I had brought with me for such an occasion, and crept down the back stairs. The Sends were waiting for me. Not in a broken-down Yugo like everyone else drove, Heinrich was at the wheel of a late model dark blue Buick sedan. I hoped no one saw me get in. He shoved it in gear and soon the car roared down the gravel road onto the paved two-lane highway.

We drove for about ten minutes, deeper and deeper into the countryside. Are they kidnapping me, I fleetingly thought? Are they Russian spies in disguise?

The conversation during the drive was casual and pleasant, mostly about the day's events and what I planned to do before I left. I was pleased to know they were inquiring about the next day, for it meant my nefarious thoughts of being kidnapped or arrested had no basis.

As the full moon rose over the hills and bathed the scene in a white glow, we passed a small village, but no one was about. In the distance farm houses and barns dotted the landscape, but no lights were on. All was shrouded in darkness. The eerie silence I observed outside contrasted to the joyful feeling inside the car. My hosts were eager to show me something, I sensed, but I had no idea what it could be.

Chapter Eleven: The Surprise

J ust as I wondered where we are going, Heinrich turned onto a narrow dirt road. A few minutes later we passed a large meadow. Cattle grazed as the last rays of sun disappeared behind the forested hills. They saw the car and followed, heading for the barn straight ahead. Did they sense something special, I thought, as I watched them amble along a well-worn path.

A large house, constructed of stone and logs, came into view. Manicured fields surrounded the house, and a garden ablaze in vivid colors lined the pathway leading to the front porch. From the looks of the impressive property, Heinrich was a successful man, not at all what I expected after hearing him speak of the hardships of the occupation.

The car came to a halt. I got out. Charlotte told me to close my eyes and led me by the arm up the steps to the front door. The uneasy feeling returned, but I went along with the ruse, as deep down I did trust them.

"You can open your eyes now," she said with a hint of glee in her voice.

I was in the middle of a large rustic room. Looking around, I saw handsome leather couches, a marble-topped coffee table, and bookcases filled with family photos and porcelain collectables. The walls were decorated with paintings of snow-capped mountains and scenic valleys. In the far corner, a chandelier made from deer antlers hung from the wood-beam ceiling, casting diffused light over a large dining table in the corner. Through a stone archway I glimpsed knotty pine cabinets decorated with hand-painted folk art designs. I guessed Charlotte was the artist, as earlier she had told me she liked to paint. An imposing fireplace stood in the other corner.

Was this what they wanted to show me? What they were so secretive about? Impressive yes, but not a reason for all the mystery.

"May I take your coat? Heinrich's voice was eager yet controlled. "I want you to feel comfortable. You are a most welcome guest." His eyes lit up as he said, "I can't wait to show you why we brought you here."

I had no idea what he meant, but nodded as I looked around the open space which served as their living room, dining room and kitchen. I had never seen a plan like this, but I liked it.

When he saw the look of wonder on my face, he said, "Many German homes are constructed like this. Much more practical to heat one large space in the winter than many small closed off rooms." It made sense. I wondered if I could find a plan like this back home.

"Come this way," he said as he slid back a bookcase near the kitchen revealing a door. Now my curiosity was piqued. Although still somewhat suspicious of his motives, I had come this far on pure faith, so no need to get cold feet now.

He unlocked the door with a key hanging from the back of the bookcase and led me down a flight of stairs, lit only by the flashlight he was holding. My imagination was running wild. What will I find down here? What was he so anxious to show me? Why didn't he turn on a light so I could see my way?

I half expected to feel a sharp pain on the back of my head, or be grabbed by invisible hands as I stood in the dark at the bottom of the stairs. Heinrich disappeared into the blackness. I heard voices. Who else was down here? I was scared. Panic set in. I could feel my heart pounding in my chest as I tried to make some sense of this mystifying situation.

Suddenly the room was ablaze. I closed my eyes for a second because of the brightness. When they adjusted, I was in a large room which looked more like a tavern than a basement. My ears picked up faint sounds of jazz riffs by Ella and Satchmo coming from a speaker in the corner. Lights flashed from a garish pinball machine, adding unexpected color to the room. An impressive oak bar dominated the space. Mounted behind, a blue and gold Pabst Blue Ribbon Beer sign flashed on and off. To complete this scene, an American flag stood in the corner. I gasped as I try to make some sense out of this bizarre sight. What was this all about?

"As you can see," he trumpeted while pouring me a stein of beer from the tap behind the bar, "I'm a closet capitalist." I relaxed and nodded at last I understood.

"I love everything American. But I have no one to share my secret with." Was this why he tried to befriend me to at the hotel, I thought, as I took a welcomed sip from the frosty glass.

"You're the first American I've met in a long time I could trust." His comment surprised me.

"You must understand the risk I am taking by showing you my secret."

I agreed.

"If my neighbors or the police knew of this room, I could be arrested for treason."

Finally, it was beginning to make sense. The Send's knew I was staying for just a few days, so they had to make their plans quickly. By chatting with me a little each day, they sought to gain my confidence, hoping I would trust them enough to come with them. So that's what the whispering was all about in the dining room.

As we sat at the bar and enjoyed a few beers, I worked up the courage to ask Heinrich about those difficult war years. His face changed. His voice grew deeper and more serious.

"When I was drafted," he slowly began, "I was sent to the Special Language School in Nuremburg to become a translator, studying both English and French."

"That explains your excellent English."

"Yes, my training was thorough. After six months of total immersion I had almost lost my accent." I agreed, for when we first met, I thought he might be British.

"At one point, the Nazis planned to drop me behind enemy lines, but then my orders were changed, and I was sent to headquarters in Berlin to decode Allied transmissions. Meanwhile, Charlotte returned to Dresden and resumed her career as a nurse. She was not allowed to follow me to Berlin."

"Were you separated long?" I asked, not wanting to pry too much.

His eyes grew moist as he told me the rest of the story.

"Yes, until the end of the war, almost five long years. At first we were able to communicate with each other, but as the war grew more intense, fewer calls and letters got through."

His voice became more choked as he continued.

"The Nazis tightened the noose around Berlin, until we were cut off from each other."

I could see sadness in his eyes as he continued to describe those difficult years. With no word from his wife for years, he didn't know if she was dead or alive.

When he heard Dresden had been bombed, and realized the war was swiftly coming to an end, he fled Berlin. He threw away his uniform, stripped clothes from a corpse on the side of the road, and tried to blend in with others who were fleeing the city disintegrating before their eyes. The Americans were advancing from the West and the Russians from the East. He knew the Third Reich's days were numbered.

He headed south and joined the throngs of refugees seeking safety in the surrounding villages. When he reached the outskirts of Dresden, all he saw was death and destruction. Falling to his knees, he wept, certain his wife had perished in the firestorms of those terrible February nights.

Smelling the charred air, he saw much of the city still in flames. The blare of wailing sirens pierced his ears and deafened his senses. He walked for miles, climbing over bodies and debris that choked the roads. Streams of people crawled out from under the rubble of their once regal apartments. Burdened with anything salvageable, they joined the endless procession attempting to leave the city. The hopelessness in their eyes haunted him for years.

The roads were clogged with jeeps, trucks, carts, wheelbarrows, wagons, anything that could carry precious cargo, all inching their way to safety. Rumors of the advancing Russians and the atrocities they committed on the helpless Germans struck fear in the hearts of the survivors. If only the Americans could get here first, was a hope whispered among the refugees.

A tip from another escaping soldier told Heinrich to look for his wife in the temporary hospitals set up in the countryside, far from the raging fires still engulfing the city. Taking the soldier's advice, he wandered from camp to camp and hospital to hospital, desperately searching for any clue to fuel the hope his wife was still alive.

He had almost given up when he saw an ambulance parked in front of a small stone cottage in a field not far ahead. Fighting his way through the maze of people lined up outside seeking medical help, he burst through the door.

The horror greeting him made him sick to his stomach. The smell of burnt flesh and death was everywhere. Temporary beds stuffed into every available space were populated with bodies covered in blood-soaked bandages. Doctors and nurses frantically raced from bed to bed tending the maimed and wounded. Behind a sheet hung between two poles to provide a modicum of privacy, a temporary operating room had been set up in the corner. Bags of life saving plasma dangled precariously from a coat hanger nailed to the ceiling.

Out of the corner of his eye he saw a petite young nurse tending the wounds of a mother holding a crying infant in her arms.

"Charlotte!" he screamed. At hearing her name she stood up and tried to figure out in all the chaos where the voice was coming from.

"It's me, Heinrich," he shouted from across the room. Unable to believe what she heard, she clawed her way through the maze of beds to a figure cloaked in mud and dressed in rags. When she recognized him, she threw her arms around his neck and wept.

"I thought you were dead," she stammered, barely able to get the words out between her sobs.

They stood in the middle of the room locked in an embrace, afraid to let go lest they would be separated again. As all watched this heart-warming scene, each hoping their loved ones would return, one of the nurses approached and said she would take over for a few minutes while they had a chance to get reacquainted.

"Arm and arm we walked out into the cool fresh air," Heinrich said as he wiped a tear from his eye. "We haven't been separated since."

After taking a long sip of beer, he composed himself, stood up and proudly stated, "As soon as I could afford it, I bought that little farm house, enlarged it and named it '*Charlottenheim*,' Charlotte's home. You are standing in it right now."

I could hardly believe what he had just told me. Wiping the tears from my eyes, I thanked him for sharing such a painful yet beautiful part of their lives.

Soon Charlotte appeared with a freshly baked chocolate cake and a beaming smile. She was as pleased as he to share their secret life with me.

"Not even my daughters know the truth of this room," Heinrich confided, changing the subject. "When they visit, I hide everything. They seldom come down here anyway."

Taking another sip of beer, he went on to say, "I don't know if I can trust them. They grew up under communist propaganda, which I am afraid did an excellent job of indoctrinating them."

What a tragedy, I thought, as I considered having to keep such a secret from my family. I couldn't imagine a government who prided itself on teaching children to spy on their parents.

To change the subject, I asked if I could get something out of the car. He seemed puzzled, but showed me the way up the stairs.

When I returned, I handed Heinrich a small package. His face lit up as he opened it, revealing the carton of Marlboro cigarettes I had brought with me from the States.

"How did you know this was my favorite brand?" he queried. "I haven't had an American smoke since my last business trip to Berlin when a colleague smuggled a pack from London. Will you join me?"

"Thanks, but I don't smoke anymore. I quit several years ago when I started grad school. Not good for singers," I quipped. "I saw you light up the other night outside the hotel and thought you might enjoy them."

Charlotte, all the while, was fussing over a small table in the corner. Soon we were invited to have dessert. She had laid out her best china, finest silver and a bouquet of multi-colored flowers graced the center of the table.

Handing me a huge piece of cake smothered in whipped cream, she said with a twinkle in her eye, "We call it *Kuchen mit Schlagoobers*. I snickered at the funny sounding name and thanked her for her gracious hospitality, and for the cake. I was in heaven. My favorite dessert.

"Now that we are safe in our little hideout, won't you to tell us something about yourself?" Heinrich leaned back, lit a cigarette and took a long slow draw.

Soon the questions came fast and furiously. He wanted to know about life in the US. As I tried to answer his many questions, I sensed he was having a hard time believing what I was telling him.

"Imagine being able to choose your own profession, go to any school you wish, travel anywhere you want, even visit a communist country." He just couldn't believe it.

I could tell by the look in his eyes, if I continued, my answers might be too painful for him.

Blowing a smoke ring into the air, he added, "It has been so long since the war and the occupation, I can't remember anymore what it is like to be free. That's why I built this room—to keep the dream of freedom fresh and alive for us."

For the next hour we exchanged stories of friends, family, travel. I tried to think of any detail which might interest them. Charlotte was anxious to hear about my childhood, while Heinrich asked questions about politics and government, noting I was much more positive about the future than he was.

"Yes, you will see the Iron Curtain come down."

"Do you think so...in my lifetime?"

"Yes definitely," I assured him. "Although the cold war seems stagnate now, I do see signs of thawing on the horizon."

"I hope you are right, but I don't see any," he said blowing another smoke ring.

I asked if he knew of the recent prisoner exchanges, or of Khruchev's scheduled visit to the United States next year?

"I don't think he would risk a visit unless there was some kind of détente in the works. Neither country can withstand the huge costs of their ever growing military-industrial complex."

"I wish I had your optimism," Heinrich retorted.

"We are spending ourselves into oblivion. Now that each superpower has hundreds of nuclear warheads, if either attacks, then mutual destruction is assured." He agreed.

"With the power to wipe mankind from the face of the earth, I don't think Russia or the United States is going to entertain that option. We just have to hope cooler heads prevail."

"Do you think Russia will ever give up her colonies?" Heinrich remarked with a new sadness in his voice. "Because that is what we have become. She uses Germans, Poles, and Czechs as a cheap labor force to rebuild war-torn Russia."

His voice grew quiet. "Rumors of whole families disappearing overnight frequently circulate. People have reason to be fearful." Now I was quiet, for I had no idea this was still happening.

"I appreciate the leap of faith you took to come here. We are grateful for your trust."

"I did notice how quiet people were on the trains and in the streets. No one spoke more than a few words. Coming from noisy Vienna it was quite a shock to experience such silence in the midst of crowds of people."

"Perhaps you can understand why," Charlotte joined in. "People are paranoid. Afraid their conversations might be overheard, or they may say something incriminating. Weren't you hesitant at first to speak to us?"

"I certainly was," I confessed. "I had been warned by the US Embassy not to speak to strangers. To be leery of anyone trying to strike up a conversation in a public place, as "ears" were everywhere. But you were both so kind, soon I felt I could trust you." They smiled.

"Thank goodness my instincts were correct, or else I wouldn't have dared come. I have so enjoyed meeting you and having this conversation."

While glancing at my watch I added, "But I'm afraid it is time to get back to the hotel before it closes. I don't want to arouse suspicions for you or me."

I finished every morsel on my plate, took my last sip of coffee and thanked them for such a memorable evening, one I will treasure for years to come. We exchanged addresses. He cautioned that my letters would be censored and to be careful not to say anything which could incriminate either of us. His letters might not even get out of the country, so not to be discouraged if I didn't hear from him right away.

The drive back was quick. After hurried hugs, and promises to meet again, I raced to the hotel and quietly made my way up the back stairs, being careful no one saw me.

In the safety of my room I reflected on the events of the evening. What had I just experienced? My answer, a brave couple hanging on to the echoes of freedom they once enjoyed before the war. By transforming their basement into a bastion, in their words, "of capitalism," they kept alive the hope of freedom so deeply embedded in them. I felt proud to have found the courage to go with them, yet sad that they had to live in such a closeted way. Imagine having to keep the charade from their daughters? To think they trusted me, a stranger, more than their own family, what a cross to bear. Luckily for me, I was the one they felt comfortable sharing their secret with. I could take this rich memory, along with countless others, back home as souvenirs of this remarkable adventure.

While drifting off to sleep, I uttered a fervent prayer for all the people I had met in this tragic city, for their courage, their well being, and for the dream of seeing their country free again. With tears in my eyes, I recounted my blessings, which I knew more than ever now I took for granted. Never again, I promised myself. Never again!

Chapter Twelve: Exploration

The next day I awoke with a strange feeling of hope, why I don't know, but it did seem somehow real. My train didn't leave until late afternoon. I had the whole day to explore. After a hearty breakfast, I packed, checked out to the hotel and took a taxi to the train station. I left my suitcase with the clerk behind the cluttered desk, and set out to explore the old city. He didn't seem altogether trustworthy, so I kept my briefcase, camera, journal and all my precious notes with me.

The day was cool yet sunny, perfect for exploring. I felt such excitement contemplating what I might see and do on this my last day in Dresden. Retracing the steps I took the other afternoon, I headed in the direction of the river. Along the way, I stopped to take some pictures. I noticed several people staring at me. I felt uncomfortable and tried to act natural.

Soon, a few curious people edged closer. I asked if I could take their picture. At first they seem frightened, but then nodded. I stepped back a few feet to frame them with the drab apartment buildings in the background. As soon as I took the picture, I pulled out the film and held it in the palm of my hand up to the light. They came closer and watched. Their eyes grew wide as seconds later an image appeared on the once blank paper. They gasped. I passed the picture around for all to see.

Why the astonished look on their faces? Then it dawned on me, they had never seen a Polaroid camera before and were amazed at the miracle of instant photography. I brought enough film with me so I took several more pictures and gave one to each of them. Thanking me, off they went, stopping ever so often to admire themselves in the photo. I put the camera back in my briefcase, smiled and continued my walk. What a delightful encounter.

Moments later, two Russian soldiers crossed the street and headed in my direction. My heart started to pound. My palms were clammy. Instinctively, I reached inside my coat pocket for my papers and handed them to the taller of the two. He didn't seem at all interested. Instead he grabbed my briefcase and tried to open it. When he couldn't, he gestured for me to do it. Setting the case on the ground, I dialed the combination on the lock and lifted the lid.

"Was IST das?" he shouted, as he bent over and removed the black rectangular box he spotted.

I tried to explain it was a camera, and showed him a few photos I had taken. From the look on his face, I could tell he didn't understand.

"Here, I'll show you how it works," I attempted to communicate. Taking the camera from him, I motioned for the two to stand close together. My hands were shaking, but I managed to focus the lens and press the button. I took the film out of the camera and held it in my hand. They came closer and watched with wide eyes. I judged one was about 6'3", in his middle forties and in very good shape. In my mind I nicknamed him "Boris." The shorter one, much wirier, had the ruddy complexion of one who drinks a lot of vodka. I called him "Ivan."

Removing the cover paper, I showed them the image. Their faces changed from scowls to smiles. As he patted "Boris" on the back, "Ivan" made a remark which set them both off. Maybe he said something like, "You sure are ugly." They exchanged jibes and then turned back to me.

"Wunderbar," Boris exclaimed and motioned me to take another picture, but much closer. I framed their faces with just a hint of the street behind them, pressed the button, and as quickly as I took the film out, snapped another picture. That instinct turned out to be a stroke of genius, for the photos seemed to satisfy their curiosity. They each took one, thanked me, and ambled back across the street, muttering to each other.

Much relieved, I put the camera back in my briefcase and continued toward the river. From the way things were going, I guessed this day was going to be a series of unique encounters, hopefully as pleasant as the last two.

The area around me, comprised of vacant lots and large imposing apartment complexes, had not yet recovered from the war. The sight was bleak. Absent were stores, restaurants, parks, playgrounds, anything

101

which gives a neighborhood a sense of community. Few people were on the street. An eerie quiet settled over the blocks and blocks of government housing I passed. Where were the children? Why aren't they out playing on such a beautiful Saturday morning?

Several blocks later, I came to a massive building the USSR constructed for fairs and exhibitions—the *Kulturpalast*. The glass façade, decorated with GDR and Russian flags hung from the roof, was imposing. Lines of people stood outside, waiting to see some Soviet sponsored event. Several cars, mostly Russian built Yugos, were parked in the lot in front.

Just past the *Palast*, I came to a large square encircled by once elegant but now bruised buildings—the *Altmarkt*. Before the war the center of shopping and a bustling open air market, it was now deserted. I crossed the street to get a closer look.

Beneath faded awnings were stores, shops and galleries, their owners outside trying to entice the few people milling around to enter and buy. As my eye traveled to the apartments above the shops, I was struck by what I saw. The windows were boarded up and the walls pock-marked, constant reminders of the ravages of war.

The sole bit of glamour in the square was a hotel trying to put on an elegant face. In front, tables draped in pressed-white cloths, teetered on broken sidewalk tiles. Uniformed waiters stood at attention awaiting customers. The hotel was a sad reminder of what once was. I wondered who could stay there? Certainly not me. "Foreigners were forbidden," I heard the voice of the embassy agent ring in my ear. Behind the hotel were the remains of the once graceful spire which crowned the *Kreuzkirche*, the Church of the Holy Cross, the oldest church in Dresden. No longer a cultural landmark, now just a bombed-out shell. Will it ever be rebuilt?

I knew I was not allowed to enter the stores, but I stopped anyway to admire the few objects displayed in the windows. At the door to what appeared to be a souvenir/curio shop, I peeked to get a glimpse of what was inside.

"*Bitte, Kommen Sie hierein,*" Come in, please, I heard a loud, jolly voice say. I tried to explain to the shopkeeper I was a foreigner, an *Auslander*, and not permitted to enter, but he took my arm and said, "*Nein, kommen*

Sie." So in I went, hoping the shop was not hiding Russian officers or German police.

As I looked around the room, it was empty of people and merchandise. I spotted a table in the corner. On it were some books about Dresden which looked interesting. Perhaps I can buy some of these I thought? Next to the table was a bin of LPs. One caught my eye. On the cover was a view of the *Hofkirche* as it looked in the 18th century, a copy of the famous painting by the Italian artist Canaletto. Not only did I love the scene on the cover, but the LP was a recording of Bach's *B minor Mass* by the *Dresden Kreuzchor* and *Staatskapelle* (Choir of the Church of the Cross and the Dresden State Orchestra). I hoped to conduct this masterpiece one day, and knew it held great significance for both Bach and Hasse. What a great souvenir this would be!

I grabbed several books and the record, paid the owner with the few marks I had left, and hurried out the door, hoping I wouldn't be seen by prying eyes.

Although I tried to be inconspicuous, my cover was blown when the owner's booming voice yelled out, *Wiedersehen und danke.* I waved faintly, lowered my head and quickly crossed the street. Stopping at a large monument in the middle of the square, I sat down on the steps and took a deep breath. Had I just broken every rule in the book? Was I being watched or tailed? I couldn't shake the paranoia I felt being behind the Iron Curtain.

When it looked like the coast was clear, I snuck out of the square and continued toward the river. Straight ahead I saw the *Bruhlsche Terrasse*, an exquisite promenade near the river designed by one of Dresden's most renowned 18th century architects. Now restored to its former glory, it was further proof of the magnificent legacy this city once enjoyed. The wide walkways, sculpted balustrades, graceful steps and small manicured gardens were a welcome sight after seeing so much destruction and decay. It was a peaceful scene. Benches lining the river front were occupied by young couples quietly talking. The only other activity on the river was a coal barge disappearing under the *Augustusbrüche*, the bridge joining the old city to the new.

In the distance I saw the remains of the Semper Opera House. Built in 1841, once it was one of the most important concert halls in Europe until it was flattened by the war. Many Wagner and Strauss operas were premiered there. Now boarded up and a shell of itself, she stood stoically in the large cobblestone plaza overlooking the Elbe, begging to be restored to her former prominence.

I continued down the river front, crossed the square and stopped dead in my tracks. I was shocked by what I saw. In front of me was the bombed-out ruins of the church I was hoping to find, the *Hofkirche*, the royal church, once the center of court life in Dresden.

I walked around to the back and noticed a door ajar behind a stack of stones and bricks piled up next to the wall. I cleared away some of the debris, forced the door open, and entered. No hint of its original splendor survived. The walls were black with soot, the windows blown out by the blasts, and the interior gutted by fire. The roof had caved in and lay scattered on the floor. Light streamed in through gaping holes in the walls and played eerily on the charred remains. I sat down on a pile of stones in stunned silence and took in the scene.

Gone were the white marble columns, the gilded altar, and the paintings by great masters which once adorned the side chapels. Gone the legendary Silbermann organ, the tall graceful Gothic windows, the great stone communion table and polished tile floors. It was all gone. No longer a house of God, once home to Dresden's small but important Catholic population, once the site of state weddings and funerals, of royal visits, of Hasse's music, it was now just a pile of rubble, home to the rats I saw scurrying about.

As I looked at the ruins I fought back tears. I was shaken. Would this magnificent church ever come to life again? I closed my eyes and imagined standing in the organ loft conducting Hasse's music during a high mass, dignitaries of the city present. What a dream it would be.

I left as quietly as I had come, hoping no one had seen me. Once outside, I took a deep breath, wiped away the tears and hurried away. Still a glorious day, I was glad to have ample time left to explore.

Several blocks away, I saw the *Kronentor*, the main entrance to the *Zwinger* Palace, and quickened my pace. I entered through the imperial gate surmounted by an imposing gilded crown and stopped to take in the scene. What a contrast to the drab sameness of blocks and blocks of Soviet post-war construction. Here was opulence and majesty on a scale only *Versailles* could rival.

The central pavilion was flanked by ornate galleries encircling colorful geometric gardens. A waterfall cascaded into a pool of playful nymphs. In perfect Classical style, each ornate building was balanced with its exact copy to form a harmonious whole. The detail in the carved pillars, the sculptures crowning the roof, the symmetrical rows of windows, all testified to the ideal of proportion and perspective.

No wonder the people of Dresden demanded the government restore this 18th century gem to its original glory. They could not bear the disgrace of seeing it razed, only to be replaced with a hideous shrine to soldiers they were told liberated their city. The *Zwinger* was a symbol of the art, beauty and elegance which had defined Dresden for centuries. Everywhere I looked was grace and harmony, no flower bed neglected, no lawn unattended. All was in perfect order. How ironic that just outside these walls the rest of Dresden was rotting away due to decades of neglect.

The museum I wanted to visit was located in the central pavilion. I climbed the steps leading to the entrance. In front was a kiosk with pictures of the palace before it was restored. What I saw shocked me. After the blitz, all was in ruin. The elegant statues had toppled from their perches and lay broken on the ground. The gardens were strewn with weeds and debris. Only an empty shell of the once ornate palace remained. Seeing those pictures made me again come face to face with the horrors the people of Dresden endured. Standing in front of me now was testimony of the will of the people who stood up to authority and demanded their "palace of honor" be restored to its former glory.

Inside, the foyer of marble floors and mirrored walls led to the Master's Gallery, home to works by artists such as Van Dyck, Vermeer, Rubens, Titian and Rembrandt. The next room contained paintings and art objects from the reigns of Augustus the Second and Third. Displayed in glass cases were handwritten letters, state documents, medals of honor, and gifts from royalty, all from the period which most interested me.

Along one wall hung portraits of the royal family, imperial commanders and court dignitaries. From my research, I recognized some names, but most were unfamiliar.

One portrait looked familiar. I knew I had seen that face before. Coming closer, I read the inscription. Painted in 1740 by the court artist Balthasar Denner, the elegant portraiture was of Hasse, dressed in a red velvet vest, white ruffled blouse, and crimson coat. At the time of the painting, Hasse had been court composer for seven years. He was at the height of his power. Noble and confident, wearing a white wig and slight smile, he looked like an amiable man, one admired by the court, his musicians and his adoring wife Faustina. He was the embodiment of an 18th century gentleman.

I gazed at the painting for several minutes trying to absorb his personality, trying to get inside the man himself. What was he like? Was this painting a charade much like the stilted portraits hanging next to him, or was he as kind as he appeared in Denner's painting? More research, digging and translating would tell, but at least I had this image to hold in my imagination as I continued to unearth facts about him and his life. I knew the book Dr. Reich had given me would be a valuable source, for it chronicled life in the theater and court during the time Hasse was *Kapellmeister*, the chief director of music.

I wandered around looking at display cases filled with wigs, glasses, pens, fans, all objects owned by members of the royal court. One case contained objects from the funeral of Augustus the Third. It was for his memorial service Hasse composed the *Requiem Mass* I discovered. An etching caught my eye. It showed Augustus lying in state on a funeral bier surrounded by tall black tapers. The walls and statues were draped in black. A procession of mourners encircled his casket. How I would love to have a copy of that etching. I grabbed my camera and took a quick shot. Hoping no one had seen me, I hurriedly stuffed the camera in my briefcase and ran to the next room.

"*Bitte, wo ist der Herren, die Toiletten?*" I asked the guard in my most polite German.

"*Geradeaus dan links,*" straight ahead to the left, he replied in a tone befitting his neatly pressed uniform. Once inside the men's room, I ducked into a stall, closed the door, and quickly pulled the film out of the camera. I was afraid I had waited too long. After several minutes, the image appeared. Though not perfect, at least I caught the gist of the scene, and would be able to reconstruct it in more detail once I returned home.

For the rest of the afternoon I visited other collections which attested to the wealth and power of the rulers of Saxony. The Armory displayed weapons from the 15th to the 18th centuries. The next room contained royal coaches decorated in pearl and gold. Hand painted dishes and silver tableware were exhibited in the Porcelain Gallery. No wonder artists and musicians from all over Europe were eager to be employed by Augustus, this most benevolent patron of the arts. During his reign, 1734-1763, his court became the envy of Europe, and the music Hasse composed, his hand-picked *Kapellmeister*, was the jewel in his crown.

I tried to imagine an orchestra playing in the mirrored ball room with its polished floors inlaid with exotic woods; or a production of a Hasse opera, in the pavilion's manicured gardens, starring his wife Faustina. After the performance, fireworks would light up the sky as torch bearers guided the royal guests back to their awaiting carriages. Each day would be filled with as many delights as could be imagined: ballet one night, opera or chamber music the next, pageants and plays during the day, with magnificent culinary fêtes before and after. Every sense was satiated. Augustus was known for his reputation of going from "pleasure to pleasure." The duty of the staff and court artists was to feed this all-consuming appetite for the new, the unusual, and the exotic.

I left the sanctity of the Palace and once more was thrown into the chaos of post-war Dresden. There was one more stop I wanted to make before boarding the train back to Vienna, and it was on the way back to the station.

From the main street I followed a small alley to the *Neumarkt*, a large square similar to the *Altmarkt* but much busier, with more stores and restaurants to choose from. I did not stop to look around, but went straight ahead and down an even smaller street to the right.

As I turned the corner, I saw the site of the *Frauenkirche*, (Church of Our Lady,) once the center of Lutheranism in Saxony. Still standing in front was the statue of Martin Luther, the leader of the Reformation who had once preached there. Designed by 18th century Dresden architect George Bähr, the church once boasted a dome to rival St. Peter's. Now it lay in ruins, the result of a direct hit during the last bombing raid. One fragment of the wall still remained, and it is here on the anniversary of the bombing that thousands of Dresdeners gather with flowers and candles and stand in silence to honor the dead.

Even though the Soviet backed government decreed the ruins remain untouched as a memorial to the victims of the war and as propaganda against the West, there was growing world-wide sentiment to rebuild the church. The sight of this once magnificent structure now a heap of stones drove the point home to me even more vividly of the futility of war. Although a child when it happened, I still felt some responsibility for my country's brutal attack on this defenseless city. I could not shake that feeling.

Time was getting on and I didn't want to be late for the train, so I took a quick picture and left, still feeling the weight of the horror of war on my shoulders. Maybe, someday the world will come together and help this war-torn city restore her monuments; at least, that was my prayer.

By the time I reached the station, I had a half hour before the train from Berlin was to arrive. I retrieved my luggage, sat down on a bench near the tracks and tried to record some thoughts and impressions in my journal. Although I had taken copious notes of the music I discovered, I had yet to reflect on the trip as a whole. From a research standpoint, the trip was a great success. On a personal note, I had met some remarkable people. From the standpoint of culture, I had a glimpse of what once was. Historically, I was beginning to get a picture of life in the court of Augustus, and as a tourist, I had some life-changing experiences. Someday I will write about this, but now was neither the time nor the place. My hand would not move; my heart was too heavy.

Chapter Thirteen: The Return

At 4:15 the train pulled into the station and I boarded for the five hour trip back to Vienna. Again I had a window seat in an almost empty car. Before the train departed, my papers were checked and my ticket validated. At least no drama this time, I thought, as I reclined in the soft leather seat and closed my eyes for a quick nap.

As soon as the train began to move, I woke up and pressed my nose to the window, anxious to see as much of this city I had grown to love. The route along the Elbe took us south and into the countryside. I thought I saw Heinrich and Charlotte's farm in the distance, and so said a fond thank you to the Send's for their unexpected gift of friendship and hospitality.

In no time we reached the East German border and I readied myself for the inspection by the guards. When the train stopped, a GDR officer came aboard and demanded I open my suitcase. He went through every item, including the bag of dirty clothes. When he was satisfied, he picked up the briefcase and tried to open it. I unlocked it for him. Inside, he spotted the books, the LP, the pamphlets and brochures.

Then his eyes lit on one object. He grabbed the black box and began shouting.

"What is this? Why did I have it?"

When I told him it was a camera, his questions came so fast I hardly had time to think of an answer. I was afraid he was going to confiscate it, but after showing him the pictures I had taken, he seemed satisfied and handed it back to me.

Next, he demanded to see receipts of the items I purchased. He made me empty my wallet to make sure I didn't have any East German Marks. I stood up, hoping he wouldn't notice my shoes where I had hidden a few as souvenirs, along with enough Austrian shillings to get me back to the hotel. I feigned poise and confidence. I had been through this before. At last, he turned his attention to the other passengers. Whew! That was a close one.

While I was being hassled, another officer searched under the seats, in the toilet, and dismantled the ceiling panels. He took off each large metal plate one by one until he was satisfied no one was hiding there. Outside the window I saw other officers shove large mirrors under the carriage of the car, hoping to thwart someone trying to escape. How desperate would you have to be to cling to the undercarriage of a train in hopes of gaining freedom? Now I understood the answer to my question. If I lived in the hopeless netherworld behind the Iron Curtain, I too might be that desperate to escape.

The train rolled ahead a few yards to the Czech border. The same charade was repeated. The Czech guards came on board and demanded passports and visas. Again the car was searched. What could have changed in a few yards to warrant another inspection? This time the watch my dad had given me when I graduated from high school caught the eye of the guard. I was afraid I would have to surrender it. But he merely admired it and moved on. On the whole, the Czech guards were more civil than either the GDR or the Russians.

As the train left the border, I breathed a sigh of relief. The worst of the ordeal was over. I was one step closer to the safety of Vienna.

Not having eaten anything since breakfast, I headed for the dining car. Walking through the other cars, I realized how fortunate I was to be in one not so crowded. In car after car each seat was occupied. The overhead bins bulged with packages and suitcases. Where were all these people going? Why did they look so despondent? If they were refugees, would their new life be any better than where they came from? These thoughts filled my head as I located the dining car and took a seat. Nothing fancy, but clean, well lit and the aroma from the tiny kitchen reminded me of how hungry I was.

I ordered a Pilsner Urquell, Prague's legendary beer, and a mixed grill (various cuts of beef, pork and chicken with slaw and braised potatoes). While waiting for my order, I took out my journal and tried once more to record some thoughts. Nothing, my muse was still numb.

110

The sound of voices from a noisy couple coming down the aisle startled me. Americans I thought? Who else would be so loud? I knew they weren't Germans, judging from the way they were mangling the language. Sure enough, I was right. I recognized the accent. They were from the Deep South. A distinctive "I declare" rang throughout the dining car. I looked up. A heavy set woman with a wide-brimmed flowered hat and a smallish man with a watch fob attached to his vest trying to keep up with her, were coming down the aisle.

Why I stood up and invited them to join me, I don't know. Maybe I thought we could swap some interesting stories. Maybe they had some experiences similar to mine. Maybe I thought I could rescue the frail man from the overbearing woman he was with.

"Why I do declare Henry, look here, I think this nice young man is an American," she said as she stopped, raised her lorgnette and looked me up and down. Maybe I spoke too soon, but it seemed like the polite thing to do as they looked so flustered.

"Yes, please join me. I would enjoy your company." I regretted those words the minute I said them.

She made her ample self comfortable and Henry sat next to me to give her more room to spread out. She was as loud and obnoxious as he was quiet and submissive. An interesting couple, I thought. This was going to be a meal to remember.

As soon as she was seated, she grabbed the menu and looked at the limited options. There was a lot of "yes dear" and "of course dear" as she started telling Henry what she wanted for diner, even before the waiter came over to our table. Each request was followed with a "but I don't want any of the.........," or "make sure it is not too......" I was beginning to think this was all a mistake.

Hoping to rescue poor Henry, I attempted to introduce myself, but she interrupted, proclaiming, "We are the Dahlripples from Boca Raton, Florida. This is my husband Henry and I am Lullabelle, but you can just call me Belle."

Henry had no chance to say a word. From here on she was in charge of the conversation. As much as I tried to draw him out, she would blurt out the answer or pose another question. Years ago he had probably given up trying to be heard or exert his own personality. I felt so sorry for him.

111

I turned directly to him, "What kind of business are you in Mr. Dahlripple?" She started to answer, but I made it clear I was talking to him.

"In the antique business," he said with a hint of at least I got one sentence out before being interrupted. "Mostly import now from England and Europe and sell to other dealers. Don't do much retail anymore." His drawl was not as sharp as hers.

"We closed the shop several years ago," Belle interjected, not missing a beat. "Much more money and fewer headaches in the import business. Besides we get to travel a lot now."

During the course of the meal I learned they first lived in Atlanta where they had a very successful business furnishing some of the most "respectable" homes in the south. She was a DAR of course, and Henry was a misguided Yankee from the north. He had gone to Bates College in Maine.

"I met my darling Lullabelle there." He liked to call her by her full name.

Neither of them finished college. He was drafted and spent two years in France as a communication specialist. She moved back to Macon to be with her parents and took up interior decorating.

They reunited after Henry was discharged, got married and moved to the suburbs of Atlanta. He fell into the antique business when a friend asked if he would run the business side. He had a head for figures. Belle soon jumped in and took over the decorating part. After a few years, they bought out the partner, opened their own business then moved to Florida.

I was exhausted listening to Belle tell their life story, Henry not able to get a word in edgewise. This was going to be a very interesting evening, or was it?

"We've been in Berlin on a buying spree for a client who loves 18th century Prussian furnishings," Belle proclaimed loud enough for the whole car to hear. "We found a dealer specializing in the period. He sold us some lovely things, at a very good price, I might add."

"What a coincidence," I remarked. "My research centers in the same era."

I told them about Hasse and his relationship with Frederick the Great, including the fact his army marched through Dresden and destroyed Hasse's home. At the mention of Frederick's siege Henry's ears perked up. I thought he might finally get in a word. But as soon as he tried, Belle took over and the monologue continued.

At first I thought she was somewhat interested in my research. But not so. She used what I said as a springboard to talk more about her, all the while demanding more and more from Sebastian, our waiter.

I felt sorry for him. He had his hands full trying to satisfy the whims of this demanding woman. Never once did she utter a please or thank you or a single word of German. I tried to intervene and at least add a *"bitte"* before her next complaint. The fish was overcooked…the rolls too hard…the coffee not hot enough. On and on it went until fed up, Sebastian decided to ignore us. He was annoyed by these "ugly Americans," and I didn't blame him. I was getting annoyed with them as well, particularly her.

More than once during the meal I kicked myself for having invited them. It would have been much more pleasant and relaxing to eat in peace and jot notes in my journal. But I was stuck for the rest of the journey and I knew it.

Belle was the kind of person you did not have a conversation with, it was more like a soliloquy. I posed a short question, she gave a long answer. Henry participated by nodding. But I must admit talking with them made the time pass. Before I knew it we were in and out of Prague, this time without incident.

Soon we would cross the border into Austria. The dining car was closing. We needed to return to our seats. The Dahlripples had a private compartment, so we had to part company. We said quick goodbyes and they made me promise to look them up whenever I came to Boca Raton, which I said to myself would be never.

My one experience in Florida was several months ago. I was invited to interview for a teaching position at Florida State. My audition lasted a few days, so I had ample opportunity to experience firsthand the sweltering heat, stifling humidity, blatant prejudice and obvious caste system. After rehearsing the choir for an hour I asked one of the students why weren't there any black singers in the choir? His response shocked me. "Oh, they have their own campus on the other side of town." I crossed Florida off my wish list. No, I would not be going there anytime soon. I was heading to Arizona for my first college position, hot yes, but at least it would be dry and I would not feel like a second-class citizen because I was not from the South.

Back in my seat, I readied myself for the final inspection by the Czech guards. First, I had to open my suitcase and put it on the seat. Then I was frisked, almost to the point of embarrassment. When asked to take off my shoes I pretended not to understand, as I didn't want to be caught with the money I was smuggling out. Something caught the officer's eye. He handed back my papers, told me to sit down and proceeded down the aisle.

Relieved, I settled down for the final leg of the journey, knowing soon I would be back in friendly territory. The inspection by the Austrian guard at the boarder was routine. I knew the Czechs were much more interested in keeping me if they suspected anything than the Austrians were in letting me back in.

Soon the familiar memories of a countryside of happy farmers and laughing children filled my imagination. I breathed a sigh of relief.

Thinking of the Sends brought home how priceless my freedom was. "There but for the grace of God go I," a thought I had entertained more than once as I pondered the hopeless plight of the people I had just left. How Heinrich and Charlotte would love to hop on a train and spend a few weeks in Paris or Vienna. Now they aren't even able to travel to another city without government consent. I could not imagine having to get permission to go on a trip. I was used to getting into my car and driving anywhere I wanted, across town, across the state or across the country.

"*Wien, zehn Minuten,*" announced the porter as he went from car to car alerting the passengers we would be in Vienna in ten minutes. I gathered my belongings, put on my coat, stuffed my journal into the side pocket, and made my way toward the door.

The train eased into the vast station and came to a halt. The porter opened the door, and I stepped out into the fresh clean air, now more than ever aware of how privileged I was.

Walking alongside the tracks, I had one more reminder of the oppression I had just escaped. Pressed against the window were faces of those sealed in cars guarded by Russian soldiers. They were forbidden to disembark. They were prisoners of the state. My heart ached for them.

They were so near yet so far from getting out of the clutches of communism.

When, I thought, would all this change? When would every man, woman and child have the same freedoms I enjoyed? How long would the Iron Curtain retain its stranglehold on these oppressed people?

To shake these dark thoughts from my mind, I went into the station, found a café and ordered a shot of Jägermeister, my favorite schnapps. Anxious to feel alive again, I wanted to get a slight buzz before going back to my hotel room.

The animated conversations coming from tables around me was a reminder I was no longer in a land persecuted by paranoia and fear. Here, people were free to speak their minds, express opposing opinions and enjoy political freedom, safe from the prying eyes of the government. Were they oblivious to the fact that several hundred miles to the north or east were millions of people who would give anything to enjoy the freedoms we take for granted?

After another shot, I hailed a taxi. I was in no shape to schlep my stuff onto a tram and make my way back to the hotel. The air was fresh and cool on my face. I took a deep breath before getting into the cab.

"Where have you been?" the driver asked in respectable English.

"Just returned from several days in Dresden," I replied.

I could tell by the look on his face he was taken aback by my answer.

"When I was a boy my family narrowly escaped from Germany at the end of the war. I never want to go back there again. Too many memories."

"I understand," I said and told him why I had traveled there.

"Welcome back to Vienna," he replied as he eased up to the *Gasthaus*, my home for several more weeks.

I gave him a generous tip, picked up the key from the hotel desk and wearily climbed the narrow stairs to my room. I had forgotten how steep they were and how hard it was to hoist my luggage up four flights. Falling into bed, I was more than happy to be back, and rather proud of all I had accomplished.

Chapter Fourteen: The Invitation

After a great sleep, I awoke to joyous sounds conspicuously absent from the Dresden landscape—the pealing of church bells. The tolling reminded me I was back in Vienna. I threw on some clothes, grabbed my backpack and rushed outside, anxious to feel again the exhilaration of freedom after my somewhat harrowing experiences behind the Iron Curtain. A gorgeous Sunday morning greeted me. I had the whole day to myself. The warm sun on my face and the chirping of the birds energized me as I contemplated what I wanted to do on this glorious day.

First, I went to the center of the old city to attend mass at St. Stephen's. The *Steffl*, as the Viennese call their beloved Cathedral, is the undisputed heart of the city. A triumph of Gothic architecture, the church is a testimony of the stone mason's art. The towering edifice, with its multicolored tile roof, was an iconic sight.

Founded in the 12th century, the church had been rebuilt numerous times, most recently after World War II. Tragically, on April 12, 1945, a fire broke out, the result of Russian vandalism. Large parts of the nave were reduced to rubble and ash. Because all of Austria supported its restoration, work was completed in less than seven years. At its rededication, the Austrian president proclaimed the *Steffl* a sign of national strength, a symbol to forever erase the horrors of Hitler's dictatorship from the minds of those who had endured the brutal Nazi occupation.

Described as "the most spiritual church interior in the world" by a noted 19th century architect, I tended to agree, as I slipped through the side door and entered the vast space. Soaring arches disappeared into the expansive rib-vaulted ceiling, and light from the stained glass panels danced on the marble floor, giving the vast interior a feeling of celestial otherworldliness, the true intent of the architects. I paused and stood in awe at the sheer beauty engulfing me. Longer than a football field and at nine stories tall, the size of the church was overwhelming.

The massive organ in the rear balcony intoned the prelude, setting the perfect mood for the solemn service about to begin. I found a vacant pew near the back of the church and sat down.

After the grand entrance of the clergy during the opening hymn, the music of the "Kyrie," the first part of the mass, sounded from above. I recognized the music—Schubert's *Mass in B flat*, a work I had studied at the U of I. The choir and orchestra were seated high above. I turned around to observe the conductor. I was transported. How I longed to be part of such beauty.

The music filling the immense space was so sublime it reminded me of the feeling I experienced several summers ago while studying conducting at Tanglewood. As a memorial to Koussevitsky, the legendary conductor of the Boston Symphony and founder of the BSO's summer home, the Tanglewood chorus and orchestra gathered in a small church near the lake on a beautiful sun-filled afternoon to perform Mozart's *Requiem*. Few were in attendance, as the service was not open to the public. But the spirit of the music, the dignity of the occasion, and the pure joy of performing with so many gifted musicians made an indelible impression on me. We were there to pay homage to a great man, and as musicians, this was our way to express our admiration for his legacy. Members of his family in attendance were as moved as was I.

In contrast to the Tanglewood experience, the nave of St. Stephen's was filled to overflowing, many standing in the aisles or sitting on the floor. I chose to sit near the back so I could make a hasty exit at the conclusion of the service. My intent was to race over to St. Augustine's several blocks away to hear their music. In Vienna, masses at the major churches are scheduled at different times, so it is possible to attend more than one service on any given Sunday morning. I learned this fact from Dr. Short, and that was my plan today. I was not going to miss this rare opportunity to hear music of great masters in churches where their works were originally presented.

Though not a Catholic, I love the drama of the mass. Attending a service allows me to sit and take in the beauty of the space, and to experience the church as a house of worship, rather than a tourist stop with guides and people milling about.

Before the service ended, I exited and ran to the *Hofberg*. By now I was familiar with the streets and had no trouble finding the *Augustinekirche*, (Church of St. Augustine), nestled among the royal apartments.

As I entered the church, I could see it was built for the intimacy of the Hapsburg royalty, not for a large public parish. The royal boxes high above the altar were designed for privacy, allowing members of the court to slip back to the palace without being seen.

The church was a strange mixture of Gothic and Baroque. I looked around at the unique combination of styles and became engulfed in the aesthetic richness of this historic church. In total contrast to St. Stephen's, St. Augustine's was an intimate space, a narrow nave supported by tall graceful arches, the walls pierced with slender glass windows. The entire space was filled with sunlight streaming in and reflected by crystal chandeliers hanging from the coffered ceiling. Not dark and foreboding, but light and airy. The effect was delicate and refined, not the heavy style of the cathedral. This sacred space demanded a different kind of respect, reverence and awe.

As I sat in a wooden pew carved hundreds of years ago, my eye was drawn to the immense altarpiece behind the marble communion table. The goal of the architects was to transport the worshiper from the terrestrial to the celestial, the secular to the sacred, and they certainly achieved it in this jewel of a church.

During the opening hymn, the clergy processed with all the pomp and splendor of a papal mass. Candles, incense, banners, acolytes, the cross, the Bible and rows of robed priests made their way down the center aisle to the high altar. What a spectacle. This was worship of the highest order, a magnificent pageant which had been celebrated and reenacted for centuries.

Again, when I heard the opening "Kyrie," I recognized the music —Haydn's majestic *Lord Nelson Mass*, a work I had conducted several times and knew intimately. I turned around to see where the sound was coming from. Perched high above at the back of the church in the organ loft was a small choir and orchestra. Their music was glorious. The featured soloist soared with ease above the superb ensemble. What a magnificent sound—voices and instruments blended to perfection in the ringing acoustics of this impressive space. Mozart had conducted here, as well as Haydn, Schubert and Bruckner. I was in awe.

I could just imagine what heavenly music these walls have heard. These superb musicians, like the generations before them, recreated this legacy every Sunday morning. I was transported as I listened to music I loved performed at such a professional level. My dream job would be to conduct these great masterpieces Sunday after Sunday with talent such as this. The soloists, I later learned, were from the Vienna State Opera, and the orchestra, members of the Vienna Philharmonic. Could it get any better than this? I doubted it.

At the conclusion of the mass, I climbed the stairs leading to the organ loft. I wanted to meet Friedrich Wolf, the well-known organist/ choirmaster, and congratulate him on such an inspiring service.

When I entered the small space, I saw him seated on the organ bench, a small man in his late forties with a gaunt yet kind face.

I introduced myself, told him how impressed I was with the music, and mentioned something of my background. He seemed as anxious to meet me as I was to meet him. I asked about the music program at the church. He told me the choir sings a full liturgical mass every Sunday, and showed me the schedule for the next few months. On the list were works of Haydn, Mozart, Beethoven, Schubert, Liszt, Bruckner, and several less familiar names. When I inquired if I might attend a rehearsal, his eyes lit up.

"How long will you be in Vienna?" he asked in broken yet understandable English.

"Until the end of summer," I replied in my faltering German.

"Well then, you must come and sing with us while you are here."

Now my face lit up. "Some of the regulars are on vacation. I would be delighted if you could join us."

I could not believe what he had just said. Was he inviting me to sing with this renowned choir?

"We rehearse Thursdays at 1900 in the building next door," he went on to say, "and on Sundays we meet at 9:15. Are you a tenor?"

"Bass," I stammered, still shocked by his magnanimous invitation.

"Very good, we need basses too," he added. "I will alert Kurt our bass section leader to look for you. Can you come this Thursday?"

"Oh yes," I said with all the enthusiasm I could muster.

I floated down the stairs and into the sunlit courtyard in front of the church. I wanted to shout or jump up in the air, but the dignity of the parishioners exiting the church restrained me.

So far this summer had been one remarkable experience after another. I could not believe my good fortune. I had met generous and fascinating people, combed through libraries and monasteries, discovered valuable works of music, visited a communist occupied city, and now this —an invitation to sing with a renowned choir. It was almost too much to take in at once. I was about to have one of the richest musical experiences imaginable, one I would treasure and call upon the rest of my career.

I wanted to celebrate, and knew where to go—Café Demel, a Viennese landmark not far from the church. Founded in 1786 by the royal confectioner to the Imperial court, Demel's reputation for exquisite pastries, desserts and culinary delicacies was legendary.

A large gold sign hung over the entrance. As I approached, everything about Demel's exuded taste and luxury. Apparently, I was not the only one celebrating, for it was packed to overflowing. Determined to make the most of this experience, I sought out the *maître d'* standing at the entrance and put in my name for a table.

"There will be an hour-long wait for seating in the salon," he informed me in perfect English, "and twenty-five minutes for the larger room upstairs."

"I am not in a hurry. I would like to have a table in the salon." I relished the opportunity to spend time in this elegant ambiance.

"Perhaps you would care to wait outside," he added. "You may have a coffee, and I will call you when your table is ready." He showed me to a small table shaded by a red and white striped awning. What a continental city this is, I thought, as I took my seat.

A beautiful warm, sunny day, the street was filled with shoppers and tourists, perfect for people watching while I waited for my table. A lovely young girl in a black skirt and spotless white blouse brought me a glass of water on a silver tray and set it before me. I ordered a *mélange* (coffee with steamed milk, a favorite of the Viennese), and settled back to enjoy the experience.

For a minute I thought I was at the United Nations. I heard bits of German, English, Russian, French, Italian, and what I judged to be Hungarian or Czech from passersby as they sauntered down the narrow street. I tried to eavesdrop on what was being said. Large groups of children ran by with a tour guide attempting to corral them. Families pushing carriages or toting children too young or too tired to walk darted in and out of the stores lining this famous street.

My vantage point was perfect. I could see the main entrance to the *Hofburg*, a massive portico guarded by immense mythical giants. To my right was St. Michael's Church, a Baroque masterpiece with a legendary musical history. Mozart and Haydn had conducted there. To my left, was the *Graben*, one of the most elegant shopping streets in Vienna. I was in the very heart of the city. I reveled in it.

Minutes later my coffee arrived along with a complimentary tarte, giving me just a hint of the culinary delights which lay ahead. I took out my journal and began writing down impressions of the morning experiences. In the space of several hours I had visited two contrasting yet equally impressive churches, observed two masses, and heard two important liturgical works by Viennese masters. In addition, I had met Dr. Wolf who invited me to sing with his superb choir. What a morning!

As I waited, I reflected on the first time I visited Demel's with Dr. Short on that memorable summer tour. She had just escorted our little group through the *Kunsthistoriches Museum*, Vienna's famous art gallery, where we saw masters like Breughel, Rubens, and my favorite, Vermeer. As it was too soon for dinner yet we were hungry for something, Dr. Short said she knew just where to take us.

The minute we entered Demel's our small hunger roared to life and we sat down to a dining experience I shall never forget. The buffet table along the mirrored wall was laden with salads, fruits, meats, cheeses, quiches, and casseroles of every kind. One the opposite wall were exquisite desserts piled high on tiers of mirrored shelves.

I quickly decided Demel's would be the site of my main meal, so I loaded my plate with samples of each mouthwatering dish. It wasn't until I came to the cashier and learned each helping was priced separately, did I realize how expensive this little repast would be. I gulped when I paid the bill and muttered something like, "this is the most expensive lunch I'll ever eat."

After attending an opera performance, we laughed at how naïve we were to think Demel's was an "all you can eat buffet," like we had back home. Why hadn't I had read the candid comment in my *Europe on Five* travel book—"If you plan to eat at Demel's, bring lots of money!"

The *maître d'* signaled my table was ready and invited me inside. Just as I remembered, the interior was luxurious—gleaming granite floors, polished black and white marble tables, delicate parlor chairs with twisted iron backs, paneled mirror walls, massive clusters of lights hanging from the coffered ceiling—the room exuded old-world charm and elegance. As I gazed at the displays of cakes, pies and pastries for which Demel's was world famous, I said a silent thank you to Dr. Short.

No buffet for me, for I knew how much it would set me back. I ordered from the menu—butternut squash soup, fresh fruit salad, toasted squares of Italian ham and cheese, and for dessert their famous *Sacher Torte*, a favorite of the young Mozart, and reputed by all to be the best in Vienna.

No sooner had I sat down and ordered, when a young American couple were seated at a table nearby. When I heard them trying to make sense of the menu, which was all in German, I offered my assistance. Soon, we were exchanging travel stories, and I invited them to join me, hoping they would be more fun than the Dahlripples.

My first impression was they were a delightful couple. Mike, in his late twenties, was training to be a broker in the commodities exchange in Chicago. I had no idea what that was, but was polite and tried not to ask too many dumb questions. Barbara, his wife, was from Pittsburg. They met in Chicago where she was studying at the famous Chicago Institute of Art.

Tall, handsome, confident, Mike talked a good game and dominated the conversation. Another Belle, I thought. He went on and on about the market while I tried to engage Barbara by interjecting questions about her studies and favorite artists. When she said she loved European masters, I knew we would click.

So, between market analysis and Vermeer and Titian, the conversation continued throughout lunch. I did manage say a little about why I was in Vienna and my recent trip to Dresden, but then the conversation returned to pork bellies and wheat futures.

"You must think about investing," Mike announced.

I tried to explain I didn't have 'a pot to throw out the window,' a saying my dad often used when describing the family finances. Having just completed two years of grad school I was flat broke.

"The only pork bellies I knew of were in cans of Spam starving students like me eat," I answered, trying to interject an element of levity. By the look on his face he wasn't amused by my attempt to make a joke.

"Take your first pay check, when you do get a job," he said with a smirk on his face, "and invest in futures. By age fifty you could be a millionaire."

Yea sure, I thought. He sounded just like an Amway salesman.

"Commodities are the way to go. Their value will go up and up."

Yes, until the next market crash I muttered under my breath. From what I had seen and from what my dad had taught me, I had no faith in Wall Street.

Barbara tried to rescue me several times from his relentless chatter, but finally gave up. I longed to discuss her love of art, but no such luck. If he was this dominating with a stranger, I wondered how their marriage would survive.

He excused himself for a minute, giving me a chance to talk to Barbara. She was petite with long brownish golden hair and deep green eyes, a real beauty. She told me she wanted to be a sculpture and art historian. Her goal was to teach in a small liberal arts college where she could do both. She was in Vienna to conduct research on Dürer, the famous German artist, painter and printmaker whose works were on view just blocks away in the Albertina.

"Perhaps you know Dürer's drawing of the praying hands? You can see it and hundreds of other works there." She was piquing my interest.

"I have been spending most of my time in the museum while Mike roams around the city. As you can tell, he is very intense and single minded. Not terribly interested in anything cultural."

"Yes, I noticed," I said, trying not to snicker.

Mike soon returned and the conversation returned to the business world. There was no doubt in my mind, he will be a successful stockbroker, but I doubted if Barbara will realize her dreams.

Every bite I took was more delicious then the last, and I tried to get lost in the pleasure of this exquisite dining experience. For the next few minutes I tuned out Mike's monologue and concentrated on enjoying my food. With my first bite of *Sacher Torte*, an incredible combination of rich chocolate and tangy raspberry which melted in your mouth, I let out a sigh of contentment which stopped the conversation cold.

"You've got to try this," I exclaimed, hoping to change the topic. "This is the best chocolate I have ever tasted."

"Not a fan of chocolate," was Mike's reply. I knew I had lost again.

"In fact, not a fan of sweets of any kind. More a cheese and fruit kind of guy." His caustic remark stunned me. Was he trying to put me down, or was it just his nature?

Sensing my unease, Barbara jumped in.

"I would love to try a bite, chocolate is my favorite." The look on Mike's face was less than kind. Maybe he felt we were mocking him, when in actuality we were just expressing a common pleasure.

So went my celebratory lunch, but it was fun to have company. They were an "interesting" couple. But for the life of me I couldn't understand how they got together. What did they have in common? I was so thankful for the relationship I had with my wife. We had our love of art, music, travel, and the sheer joy of life to bind us together. Whatever this couple had was not apparent, at least not to me. I left after exchanging addresses. We promised to look each other up, which I knew would never happen. But at least I had the satisfaction of helping them taste some of Vienna's finest.

Taking Barbara's advice, I walked several blocks to the Albertina. Nestled behind the Opera House, the museum lived up to Barbara's raves. I enjoyed the rest of the afternoon admiring Dürer's masterful paintings, etchings and drawings. My favorite was an etching of a rabbit with long pointed ears. He reminded me of Thumper, a pet I had as a kid. He was gentle and playful until he got older and started to bite. My dad made me take him back to the pet store, where I was told they would find him a home. Although I often wondered what happened, I was afraid to find out, certain the truth would hurt too much. So, I just told myself he was happy living on a farm with lots of his relatives.

Chapter Fifteen: More Revelations

The next week was filled with surprises and new experiences. On Tuesday I sought out Dr. Novak at the library. I was anxious to tell him about my Dresden adventure. He greeted me with open arms, and for the next hour I shared all the discoveries I made on my brief trip behind the Iron Curtain.

"I am so impressed with your accomplishments," he stated as he stopped to refill his pipe with the sweet smelling tobacco which permeated his office. "It seems your biggest obstacle now is getting microfilms of the scores you located."

"I agree. Professor Reich warned me it would be difficult to get anything out of East Germany, especially now in this tense political climate."

"Give me a few days and I will see what I can do. I just thought of an idea which might work, but it will take some time to work out the details." What could he have in mind?

"Let's meet again next week. In the mean time, continue your research here. I will alert my staff to help you find what you need."

Thanking him for his valuable support, I walked out of his office with renewed confidence. Maybe, he might find a way to solve the sticky problem of the Dresden microfilms. I feared if I could not examine them in detail, I doubted my dissertation committee would continue to approve the topic. I had to get hold of those scores. Dr. Nowak had just given me a glimmer of hope.

Taking advantage of the added time before our next meeting, I decided to visit the other major music library in Vienna, the *Gesellschaft der Musikfreunde*. Located just off the *Ringstrasse* several blocks from the Opera House, the *Gesellschaft* was founded in 1812 by wealthy patrons. Their purpose was threefold: produce concerts, train musicians, and preserve music. Concerts were held in the *Musikverein*, an elegant yet intimate concert hall now home to the world famous Vienna Philharmonic. So prized are tickets for this ensemble, they are willed from one generation to another. Unless you know someone or have connections, it was almost impossible to hear the orchestra in this historic setting.

Armed with my letter of introduction from Dr. Novak, I entered the *Gesellschaft* and walked upstairs to the second floor where the library is located. The middle-age woman at the front desk inspected my letter with a jaundiced eye. After handing me a lengthy form to fill out, she escorted me to the main reading room. An intimate space, the narrow room contained long tables occupied by scholars pouring over scores spread out before them.

I was eager to join them, so I located the card catalogue in the far corner and began my search. Sure enough, they had two Hasse scores: *Salve Regina* for women's chorus written for the *Ospedale* in Venice, the same institution for which he wrote the *Miserere*, the piece which started me on this whole adventure. I also found reference to a work I'd never heard of—*St. Elena al Calvario*, (Saint Elena at Calvary), an oratorio for chorus, soloists and orchestra. I wondered, could Faustina have sung the lead at the first performance? Maybe my research will answer the question.

As it would take several minutes for the scores to be retrieved, I leafed through the cards to see what else I could find. I knew the *Gesellschaft* had the autograph score of the Brahms *Requiem*. Would my green card allow me to see this priceless score? I made a note of it along with the two Hasse scores and took my requests to the front desk.

"I can call the Hasse works now, but you will have to make an appointment to see the Brahms score."

I looked puzzled, so she added, "There is a waiting list for this important work." After consulting her reservation book she suggested I return at four next Thursday.

"Yes, perfect," I responded and made a note of the day and time. I could spend most of the day at the *Nationalbibiliothek* and then rush over here in time to see this priceless treasure.

At first the librarian seemed cold and distant, but she became more gracious as our conversation continued. I think the letter from Dr. Novak impressed her somewhat, so she let down her guard as watchdog of the collection.

In a matter of minutes I had the Hasse scores in hand and was struck by the difference in appearance from other manuscripts I had seen. The oratorio score was an autograph, in Hasse's own hand. At last I had a chance to observe how he put pen to paper. His hand was clean yet shaky, often difficult to decipher. Were the notes on lines or spaces? Sometimes I couldn't tell.

Although in his forties when he wrote this work, his penmanship looked more like an old man at the end of his career. Was it the result of having to write fast to complete his many commissions? At any rate it was fascinating to see an original score and compare it with the many copies I had seen.

What struck me first was how facile he wrote. The page was clean, no smudges or spills. Did Hasse work out the music in his head, or at the keyboard, and then transfer it to paper, like Mozart? Or did he first make sketches similar to Beethoven? My research, I hoped, would help me answer this and other questions which kept cropping up as I delved deeper into his music. I did know, however, I was working with primary sources, original 18th century materials, many not recently examined. I felt encouraged as more and more of Hasse's life and music was being revealed to me.

For the rest of the afternoon I studied the scores, observing both similarities and differences in his writing style. Although the orchestrations were similar to his masses, the vocal writing in these two works was different. For one thing, in the oratorio, he used dramatic recitatives to tell the story, followed by more lyric solos, often in the form known as *da capo* arias. This structure of ABA, where the first part of the aria (A) is repeated after the middle section (B), allows the singer to add embellishments. The art of improvisation was at the heart of Baroque vocal music, and Faustina's reputation for her agile and flexible technique would be perfectly suited for solos such as these.

Conversely, the church at this time condemned the practice of repeated texts, so *da capo* arias are not found in liturgical works.

The choral writing was also different in the oratorio; for the most part much simpler and sparingly used, often only at the end of an act or major scene. In the mass, the chorus had the more central role of singing texts which refer to the faithful, a technique Hasse adheres to religiously.

I loved making these observations, and realized how much of his music I had not only studied, but digested. Hasse's voice was beginning to speak to me clearer now than I thought possible. My original goal was to see if I could find his music. Now, I was becoming an "expert," at least in some people's eyes. I had to chuckle. What a preposterous idea. Yet didn't Herr Reich refer to me as such when we were identifying scores at the Dresden library? Perhaps he was right.

Soon time was up and I returned the scores to the front desk. I thanked the attendant for her assistance, adding how eager I was to spend time with the Brahms *Requiem*, a work I loved and admired. She nodded and smiled.

For the next several days I dove into the project of translating the immense amount of German, hoping it would help me unlock secrets of Hasse's life. I was determined to flesh out his biography before I left Vienna, for I knew once back in the states life would be more complicated. I could only imagine what was ahead of me as a brand new college professor.

ॐ   ॐ   ॐ

On Thursday, I returned to the *Gesellschaft* at four o'clock as planned, and checked in with the woman behind the desk. Austrians appreciate promptness.

"Please, follow me." She was more polite now.

"First, you must leave your briefcase with me. Personal items are not allowed in the Rare Book Room." I nodded I understood, placed it behind the desk, and followed her down a narrow hallway to a small paneled room. An old man dressed in a long grey smock greeted me. His uncombed hair and glasses precariously perched on the tip of his nose gave him the appearance of a monk in a cloistered monastery.

After handing me a large polished wooden chest complete with hammered brass hinges, he beckoned me to sit at the desk in the middle of the room. Silently, he retreated to his chair near the door. It was obvious he would be watching my every movement. I put on the protective gloves and carefully opened the sacred vessel.

Cushioned in red velvet, the music lay sleeping in this protective tomb. I felt I was unveiling a priceless Tiffany diamond. To the music world, this opus is much more valuable than any gemstone could be. My hands trembled as I held the original hand-written score of Brahms' *Ein deutches Requiem*, the score he used when he first conducted the work. Not only did I have a piece of history before me, but one of the world's most beloved choral works as well. I knew it intimately. I had conducted it several times.

For the next hour I poured over Brahms' score, observing notes he had written in the margins, changes he had made in dynamics, articulation, voicing and text underlay. Written before his first symphony and well before the mantel of the "next Beethoven" was thrust upon him, this work was deeply personal.

I noted with what care he set passages taken from Luther's translation of the Bible. A self-confessed humanist, Brahms chose texts for his "German Requiem" that were universal in spirit—spiritual, yes, but decidedly not creedal or liturgical.

After the death of his mother, he added another movement. As if to assuage his own grief, he lovingly set the text "I will comfort you as a mother comforts her child" for the soprano soloist in an achingly lyrical passage.

While studying this most intimate movement, I had to put down the score and wipe away tears. It was too painful to continue. My own mother had died not long before, and I felt the loss acutely, even more so when I came upon this passage.

I remember the first time I sang the work as an undergraduate before death had touched me, thinking how fortunate I was to have supportive parents, especially my mother, who encouraged me to follow my dream of becoming a musician. By the next time I sang the work, in grad school, she had died of a rare virus which took her in one night without a fight.

With the open score in front of me, I vividly recalled her death. I was living in Palo Alto and about to go to San Francisco with a friend. My grandmother phoned and told me my mother was on the floor. She couldn't move her. I called an ambulance and hopped into my car. By the time I arrived thirty minutes later, I saw the ambulance parked in front, but there was no other activity. By now she should have been on her way

129

to the hospital. Fearing the worst, I raced up the stairs to discover the door wide open.

A helpless EMT stood over her lifeless body. I was in shock. She can't be dead? I talked to her last night. We made plans to have lunch later that week. I sat down beside her and sobbed. I was too late, too late to say goodbye, too late to tell her how much I loved her, too late to thank her for believing in me, for being my best friend. To lose someone you love so much without having an opportunity to share those intimate thoughts felt as cruel as death itself. It has haunted me ever since.

At the time, I was more worried about my dad. He had been complaining of shortness of breath and could only speak in a whisper. My folks were in town so he could visit his doctor. Although my mother had a history of health issues, she suffered for years from back pain and sciatica, and had endured countless agonizing operations, her health was not in question.

Crouching over her body, I wanted to cradle her head in my arms, but I froze, not able to move. My first thought was to run from the scene, but I had to call my dad and tell him his wife had died. I couldn't ask my ninety-year old grandmother. I had to do it. I was in charge now. I had to step up to the plate. In an instant, my optimistic youth was snatched away, and I was thrust into manhood.

Moments later, I spoke with the doctor. He cautioned me about the added shock this news would be for my dad who had just been told he had lung cancer, which would require immediate hospitalization.

I reeled at the news and slumped down on the floor. What had promised to be a wonderful day in San Francisco, had turned into a double tragedy—my mother was dead and my dad had cancer. What was I supposed to do? Give him more tragic news over the phone? No, I couldn't do that. I told the doctor I would be right there. I wanted to tell my dad in person, not over the phone. I wanted to make sure he was admitted to the hospital to be treated for his physical, mental and now personal pain.

Thinking about her death brought back the sadness I experienced on that fateful day that forever changed my life. My dad lived for several years, but when he could no longer breathe, even on 100% pure oxygen, he died in his sleep. They were both in their fifties, much too young. I mourned those lost birthdays, anniversaries, and Christmases. No one loved Christmas more than my dad. Even though as a kid I felt somewhat distanced from him, he always came to life at Christmas, like a renewed Scrooge.

My parents were never allowed to grow old. For me they are frozen in time, like the picture I have of them on my dresser, standing together on my brother's porch cradling their grandchildren, beaming as they embraced this new phase of their lives. They never enjoyed those golden years of retirement, never vacationed in Hawaii, their life-long dream.

Most painful for me, I was not with either of them when they died. One day they were a major part of my life, the next day gone. I remember telling my wife when I heard news of my dad's death, "I'm an orphan now," the words so painful they barely escaped my lips. Now I had only my brother to help me remember those cherished childhood years.

Pop, as we lovingly called him, passed away while my wife and I were flying home from Illinois during the Christmas holiday break. I had just spoken with him the night before. He was in the hospital recuperating from an attack of pneumonia, but was hopeful to be strong enough to spend the holidays with us.

For some unknown reason, I started to read a book written by a high school friend. Titled *The Other Side*, it was a true account of a grieving wife trying to contact her husband who had mysteriously disappeared while hiking in the Holy Lands. He was later found lying under a ledge trying to escape the sweltering heat. He died of a stroke. He swore to her as a man of faith, for he was an Episcopal bishop, that upon his death he would reach out to her from "the other side." As a first year grad student who had not read a word not assigned, I tore into my friend's chilling account.

Something compelled me to buy the book I found quite by accident while searching for something to read on the plane. Perhaps I first picked it up because I knew the author, and then was drawn to the subject, the wounds of my mother's recent death still fresh and open.

My wife's head was snuggled on my shoulder as the plane took off, and soon she was fast asleep. But I was wide awake, eager to read more of my friend's personal story.

Halfway through the flight and well into the book, I felt a cold, dark presence pass through the cabin of the plane. What was that, I thought, and set the book down.

"Honey, did you feel anything?" I asked, waking her up.

"What?" she cooed, still in a drowsy state.

"A chill that just went through the cabin."

"What are you talking about, I didn't feel a thing. Can I go back to sleep? I was having a great dream."

I wondered, was the eerie feeling I just experienced a reaction to the theme of the book, or did I actually sense something? Was someone trying to contact me, like the author suggested? Was it my imagination? Was I so tired from a grueling semester studying day and night that I was hallucinating?

"Go back to sleep, honey. I am sorry I woke you."

It wasn't until the plane touched down in San Francisco, and we were greeted by my wife's parents in the terminal, was I told the news. Pop had died several hours earlier. The news was shocking, but the thought he died while we were in flight haunted me.

Was the dark presence I felt his way of preparing me—of saying goodbye? I felt the chill return and began to shiver. My wife put her arms around me, trying to console me as tears streamed down my face.

But that wasn't my first paranormal experience. Just after my mother's death, I had other strange feelings. Often while driving I would see her out of the corner of my eye. But when I turned my head, she would vanish. Those sightings lasted for several years. Once, I even chased a woman down the street, only to be rejected when I caught up with her and discovered the truth. My dad also told me that more than once, in a moment of loneliness, he searched his small one bedroom apartment, checking under the bed and in the closet, certain he would find his beloved wife hiding somewhere. When he confessed this to me, I realized how depressed he had become and vowed to spend more time with him as soon as I finished grad school. I never had the chance. He was gone before I could comfort him or say goodbye.

Chapter Sixteen: Back to Reality

The jarring sound of an alarm signaled the library was about to close, and I was shocked back to reality. I remembered where I was, in the *Gesellschaft*, holding the score of the Brahms *Requiem* in my hand. I felt comforted, Brahms' original intention, to comfort the mourners and bless the departed. For me and millions of others who knew and loved this work, he certainly succeeded.

After wrapping the score in its original cloth, I returned it to the attendant who had been watching me like a hawk for the past hour. He took the precious package and bade me *"Grüss Gott,"* as I left the hallowed room.

Was I different for having spent time with this masterpiece? You bet I was. I had touched a part of history and was affected by the experience. Not only the genius of Brahms, but the personal connection I had with the work, moved me deeply. I left the *Gesellschaft* feeling richer inside.

My next goal was to grab a bite before the choir rehearsal at St. Augustine's. My pace quickened as I thought about the unique opportunity I was about to experience.

Crossing the *Ringstrasse*, I headed for the *Opernplatz* where I knew I would find restaurants and coffee houses well within walking distance of the rehearsal site. As I walked, I imagined what the rehearsal would be like. From the quality of sound I heard Sunday, I knew there were many excellent singers in the choir, some with trained voices. Of course the entire rehearsal would be in German. Would I be able to understand enough to keep up? Although Herr Wolf had invited me, what would the others think of a stranger coming into their midst?

Why the hesitation? Was I trying to talk myself out of going? I knew I was skilled, had a lot of experience, was a trained musician and had a reasonably good voice, so why all of a sudden was I so nervous?

Maybe, I was just hungry and needed to quiet myself after such an emotional experience in the *Gesellschaft*.

I found a *Conditorei* near the Opera House aptly named *Aïda*, not too expensive, and with a good selection of entrees. Famous for good food and quick service, the restaurant was one of a chain scattered all over Vienna.

After wolfing down a glass of beer and enjoying a traditional *Wiener schnitzel*, I felt better, and convinced myself I was going to enjoy singing with such a talented group, even though I didn't know a soul or could barely speak their language.

At the appointed time, I entered the Sacristy next to the church and climbed the narrow stairs. Several people were ahead of me. I hoped they were going to the rehearsal so I could follow them through the maze of corridors. I saw a sign on the second floor landing—*CHORPROBE*, with an arrow pointing to the left, and headed in that direction.

The small room with chairs arranged in a semi-circle around a polished baby grand was bustling with activity when I entered. I spotted Herr Wolf. He crossed the room to greet me.

"*Grüss Gott Herr Wilson*" he said in a most pleasant way. "Welcome to the *Chorprobe*. I am so glad you accepted my invitation."

He introduced me to Kurt, the bass section leader, a tall man with a distinguished white goatee. He indicated I sit next to him as he handed me a well-worn piece of music.

With much anticipation I opened it—*St. Cecilia Messe* by Joseph Haydn, one of his large symphonic masses. I knew I was in for a rare and privileged evening.

Turning the page, I was surprised to see only my bass part. Unlike scores in the states where all voices and accompaniment are printed, European choirs sing from *partiturs*, choral scores which notate a single voice part. For example, sopranos see only their notes, and likewise the other voices as well. With no cues or references to the other parts, my score showed twelve measures of rest and then a B flat dotted half note on the top line of the bass clef. Not having perfect pitch, I wondered how I would find my first entrance, let alone the hundreds of others I would have to negotiate in this one rehearsal.

Without a vocal warm-up or announcements, Herr Wolf launched into the piano introduction as people scurried to their seats. Magically, at the twelfth measure a gorgeous B flat major chord sounded, and we began the opening "Kyrie."

At first, I struggled with the Viennese pronunciation of Latin, which tends to be Germanized. However, the voices around me were so well trained, I soon had no trouble joining in. Navigating the *partitur* was easier than I thought, and Kurt's big, rich, booming voice was easy to blend with. He made me feel very much at home.

With very little comment from Herr Wolf, we sang through the mass, pausing only to correct a rhythm or pitch, or answer a brief question. Everyone was attentive, and pencil in hand, marked their score when a comment was made. It was evident from the outset, he had the group well trained. A very professional rapport was maintained throughout the rehearsal. Never did he ask for quiet, something I found myself doing all too often with my church choir. Could I instill this professionalism in my singers? I vowed to make this a new priority. Being younger than most in the choirs I conducted, I felt intimidated that I might lose their respect if I turned into a disciplinarian. No more I thought. I was going to raise the level of rehearsal decorum and insist on a more professional working environment.

After settling in, I looked around to see who was in the choir. I guessed the average age to be around forty. The younger members were sopranos with clear light voices, not like some in my choirs with wobbles you could walk through. These singers were well trained, experienced and familiar with the music.

The time flew and soon the rehearsal was over. With instructions from Herr Wolf to meet Sunday at 9:15 in the choir loft, the singers filed out of the room.

Kurt invited me to have a beer with him. At first, I hesitated due to my limited German, but throwing caution to the wind, I accepted. At least I knew we had several things in common, our love of singing and our love of music.

We walked several blocks down the street to a little tavern with colorful lanterns hanging outside the door. By now we were five in our party, including Herr Wolf who decided at the last minute to join us. Two had a good command of English and could help me follow the conversation. We sat in a booth at the back away from street noise.

My companions had so many questions, I felt I was taking my "orals" all over again, but this time, the sweat I was experiencing was the beer moistening my lips. I also had questions, and soon learned they had sung these great works most of their lives, starting as boys with unchanged voices. The music of Mozart, Haydn, Schubert, Beethoven, and Bruckner was in their blood. It was their heritage, and they wore it like a badge of honor.

Not only were they Austrians, they were Viennese. They lived in the musical capital of the world; the city that produced more great composers than any other; the city heralded for centuries as the artistic and intellectual center of the western world; the city known for its artists, musicians, writers and philosophers.

My fellow singers were special, and they had every reason to feel so. I was honored to share this evening with them. St. Augustine's Choir was considered not only the finest in Vienna, but in all of Austria. Their treasured tradition of singing the great liturgical masterworks dated back to the 16th century and the days of the Hapsburgs.

They were curious about my education, why I was in Vienna, who was Hasse, and why hadn't they heard of him. In my limited but nevertheless enthusiastic German, I tried to explain my mission and research. They seemed not only interested, but fascinated. They hung on every word as I mentioned my adventures in Dresden, a city none of them had visited. They asked for more.

When I began to relate in detail my trip, a hush fell over the room. I realized I had experiences which even to Austrians were rare. Several had visited Munich or Frankfurt, but none dared travel behind the Iron Curtain. In their eyes, I was something of a folk hero, as I shared the many mishaps I encountered in Dresden. Of course they knew of the East German presence in Vienna, and of the Consulate, but none dared venture inside, nor contemplate a trip such as the one I had just completed.

For many, I was the first American they had spoken with. The city teamed with tourists from all over the world, and hundreds of Americans were among those who flocked to Vienna. But those not in the tourist or hotel industry had little opportunity to come in contact with them.

Americans were heroes in their eyes; the ones who liberated Austria; the ones who brought down the Nazi regime, and rebuilt much of war-torn Europe. How proud I was to represent my country to these grateful people. Never had I felt such patriotism as now.

The more I got to know the singers, the more they began to relate stories of their lives during those war ravaged years, the horrors of which I could not imagine. I had never been subjected to endless nights of bombings; nor had I witnessed senseless beatings by the brown-shirted Gestapo; nor seen family members and neighbors disappear in the middle of the night never to be seen again; nor had I stood in line for hours for a loaf of bread or a jug of milk. Life in Austria under the occupation was brutal; they were imprisoned in their own country. Condemned as sympathizers for just speaking Hitler's language, they were branded Nazis in the eyes of the world.

Few told of story-book endings like in *The Sound of Music*. Most had lost family, relatives, friends, neighbors to the war. Many were conscripted into the army and sent to faraway places to do Hitler's bidding. I was moved to tears as they related their personal stories, not out of hate or bitterness, but as a way of expressing their love for the Allied soldiers who delivered them from Nazi oppression.

Now Vienna was beautiful and proud again. Her streets no longer strewn with rubble, her buildings no longer gutted by flames, her parks no longer littered with tents and cots sheltering the homeless. She was back to the role she had played for centuries—a majestic world-class center of culture and the arts. At the end of our gathering, I proposed a toast—"to Vienna, to America, and to freedom."

Chapter Seventeen: More Surprises

Having the opportunity to stay in Vienna for an extended time was such a gift, I felt obligated to fill each day with, memorable experiences. I spent morning hours in cafes speaking to locals about life in this imperial city; frequented museums and art galleries so often as to be on a first name basis with the guards; made friends with hawkers in the *Nachtmarkt*, and chatted up waiters in my favorite restaurants. I was inhaling the sights and sounds of the city. Afternoons and evenings were spent researching, translating, and writing. The project was beginning to take shape.

My favorite activity by far was singing with the St. Augustine Choir. Each time I mounted the steps to the choir loft and sang another masterwork with their magnificent choir and orchestra, not in concert, but in the context for which it was written—a high celebratory Roman Catholic Mass—I felt I was taking a master class in choral repertoire. Every Sunday morning we sang a full mass and chanted all of the propers, the special prayers and texts dictated by the Lectionary, the church's guide to the liturgical year.

For me, a Protestant neophyte, the chants were the most challenging. These ancient melodies—Gregorian chants—were never rehearsed, not even on Thursday nights. So it was baptism by fire. During the mass, the organist gave a pitch and the men sang as one the intricate melismas and unfamiliar Latin texts. Their singing was flawless, effortless, ageless. I remember hearing their perfectly blended voices waft over the congregation the first Sunday I attended service. Now I was part of this mystical setting.

The routine was the same each Sunday: rehearse with orchestra at 9:15, break for coffee, don our robes, and sing the 10:30 high mass. The church was always packed, not with tourists, for few knew of it hidden away in the corner of the *Hofberg*. No, this was the church of the faithful, those who have worshipped in this magnificent setting for generations. St. Augustine's represented to the Viennese all that was royal and majestic—when she was the capital of an empire stretching from Eastern Europe to the new world, and home to the greatest composers and musicians of the day.

To think I was privileged to be a part of this tradition was more than humbling. I cherished every minute.

                                    ❧ ❧ ❧

Soon it was time to fly home and resume a normal life. My stay in Vienna seemed more like a dream, one I didn't want to awaken from. Here, my responsibility was to complete the research. Back home, as a brand-new college professor, a new challenge awaited me, one both exciting and yet fearful. After checking the airline schedules, I made arrangements to leave the following Tuesday. I had four days to wrap things up.

Saying goodbye to my new church friends and Herr Wolf was difficult, but saying goodbye to Dr. Novak was much more painful. Without his help and encouragement it is doubtful I would be able to continue this project, but I still had no idea how to get my hands on those Dresden manuscripts.

Approaching the library, I thought of what to say to him to express my appreciation. But as soon as I entered his office and saw him sitting in his swivel-back chair smoking his pipe, I felt nothing but love for this man. He had been like a father to me, nurturing and guiding me in his most gentle way.

He turned around as I approached. On his face was a grin new to me. "Sit down," he said with the enthusiasm of a child with a new toy. "I have some good news." I trembled as I found a chair and leaned closer to him. He had my complete attention as he read a letter just received from Dresden.

Miraculously, Dr. Reich had received permission from the East German higher-ups to send the micro-films to Vienna in exchange for several Dr. Novak possessed. Included in this exchange was a missing page from a mass I discovered in Dresden. Listed in the Vienna catalogue as an "unknown fragment," its partner was waiting in Dresden to be reunited. If Dr. Novak would send the fragment, along with other requested works to Dr. Reich, he in turn would send the films to Vienna I desperately needed. Dr. Novak would then forward them to the Reference Department of U of I library. Like two warring factions negotiating a prisoner exchange, Dr. Reich found an angle to satisfy all concerned. If either of my new mentors wanted to send me home with a gift, there was none greater than this news.

Dr. Novak arose from his chair me to give me a hug, for we both realized the importance of the letter.

"At last, communication from Dresden," he exclaimed with a new sense of optimism. "Perhaps I can establish a dialogue between our two libraries now." He was overjoyed to think a barrier which for decades had seemed insurmountable, at last had been breached.

"I have you to thank," he commented as he took another puff on his pipe. "You made this possible. Your friendship with Dr. Reich and the respect he has for you have opened new doors." Feeling unworthy of his praise, I looked down, averting eye contact.

"Perhaps, I will be able to make a trip to Dresden, maybe even to East Berlin to see my son," he added as he looked at me with soulful eyes.

I was stunned. His remarks took several moments to sink in. I came to say goodbye and thank him for his kindness. Now he was praising me for my work. It was too much to comprehend. Added to his praise was the realization the final piece of the puzzle was in place—access to the manuscripts I unearthed. For the first time it was clear— my dissertation and degree were at last in sight.

I hugged Dr. Novak again, for it was all I could think of doing. Tears began to flow as I searched for words to thank him.

"You must send me a copy of your edition," he added as I said goodbye and left his office.

"I'll not only send you a copy," I added, now grinning from ear to ear, "I'll send you an invitation to the premiere performance!"

Happier than I could have imagined, I bounded down the steps of the library into the main square and made a beeline for my favorite spot—Café Demel. I couldn't wait to savor their delectable pastries. To say I was celebrating was an understatement. The realization all my goals for this trip were accomplished was beginning to set in.

From fiction to fact, from references on a catalogue card to actual manuscripts, from hidden clues to reams of information hitherto thought unavailable, it had all been revealed to me. I was heading home with the resources needed to complete my long held dream. For the first time in ten years of pursuing graduate studies, I sensed the end was in sight. All I had to do now was put the puzzle pieces together to discover this enigmatic Mr. Hasse. By some miracle of fate, doors closed for centuries were opening, and I was the privileged one to enter.

Chapter Eighteen: Home

I stepped off the plane in San Francisco into the loving arms of my wife. She had spent the summer with her parents preparing for our move to Tucson. Cami, as I fondly called her, was as excited as I to think everything was now in place for me to complete the dissertation, and lovingly vowed to nag me until I finished it. We both knew the academic world was strewn with "all buts," and we even knew a few. After all our sacrifices, I did not want to become another statistic, so I promised on bended knee I would finish as fast as possible. Little did I realize, nor want to face, just how much work was ahead, or how long it would take.

After moving into our new home in the desert, the first of many packages from the U of I arrived. Eager to examine the music and dive into the research, I was hit with the realization I had to find a way to juggle time between full-time teaching and the project looming ahead of me. Needless to say, I knew many late nights were in store.

The home we choose, after frantically looking and almost giving up, turned out to be the perfect one. Situated in the hills above Tucson, it offered a panoramic view of the magnificent Arizona sunsets and the lights of the city from our rooftop retreat. Built in 1920, the home had large rooms, double-thick adobe walls, high ceilings, an enclosed backyard and plenty of room for expansion. Situated on four acres of natural desert growth, the site was complete with hundred year-old saguaros, stately agaves, wild harried cholas, graceful olive trees, and a tack room for our imaginary horses.

For two young, starry-eyed kids who had shared nothing but apartment life, it was a dream come true—a home of our own. Here we would put down our roots, raise a family, entertain our friends and grow old together. We awoke to roadrunners and coveys of quail scurrying along the backyard wall. At night with the stars so clear and bright you could almost reach out and touch them, we heard the cry of wolfs and the snarls of wild javelinas. It was our little paradise, an oasis from the noise and hubbub of the city. The biggest draw-back was the cost, twice as much as we had agreed upon. But with confidence only youth have, we vowed to find a way to afford it.

No sooner had we began unloading boxes from the moving van parked in the circular driveway on the first day we took possession, when the doorbell rang. Though unexpected, we had our first visitor. He introduced himself as the Senior Pastor of the church across the street from the University.

Thinking he was paying a call to invite us as newcomers to attend services, perhaps tipped off by our realtor, or by the hulking van parked in front, I tried to explain we were moving in and would to love visit, but at some other time. He insisted he needed just a minute and wasted no time getting to the point.

Dispensing with the niceties, on the spot he offered me a position—Director of Music at the University Presbyterian Church. There was no way I was going to add that responsibility to my list. Cami promised when we contemplated the move, I would not have to take a church job, at least until I finished the degree. With her standing next to me, I was sure she would back me up. I blurted out perhaps I might consider it at a later time, but definitely not now.

He didn't take my cue, and insisted I reconsider. Thinking I might scare him off by proposing some ridiculously high figure he couldn't match, I hemmed and hawed. All the while he tried to convince me I was the one he wanted for the vacated position. He had read my dossier, spoken with my former pastor and knew I was the new Chair of the Choral Department at the University. Eager to create a closer liaison between the church and the school, he proposed to sweeten the deal by offering scholarships to voice students to act as section leaders.

He had done his homework. But it wasn't until he mentioned the salary and my wife said "take it," did I realize I was trapped. The figure he quoted was twice what I had previously earned. In fact, it was the exact amount of our monthly mortgage payment. Had he been talking to our realtor? Saying yes meant we would be able to bank part of my salary and do some needed repairs on the fifty-year old house. But more important, it also meant my wife would not have to find a full-time job. The entire package was just too tempting, so I accepted.

In hind sight, it turned out to be one of the best decisions I made. I enjoyed every minute at the church. The pastor, staff and choir became some of our closest friends. True to his word, I soon had twelve full tuition scholarships in my pocket and was able to hire my most talented students as section leaders for the Chancel Choir. With so much new talent, in a matter of months a good church choir became one of the finest in the city. Attendance grew, and so did our reputation. Many from the university community, who were members of the church, were quick to comment to their colleagues, including my dean, on the superb quality of music in the service. Later, this university support would be welcomed when forces turned against me.

After all the boxes were unloaded and everything was in its place, I opened the packages from the U of I—the treasured microfilms. To examine them I used the reading machines in the university library. But this method proved so time consuming, that at this rate, I would never see my wife or have time at home. I knew I had to find a solution.

To solve the problem, I rented a micro-film reader from the local media center and set up shop in the downstairs bedroom. The hulking machine, with its enormous overhead screen, dominated the room. But there were other problems with this arrangement as well. Although the house had double-thick walls and something called a swamp cooler, neither was equipped to offer relief from the desert heat which often rose to triple digits and rarely cooled off at night.

After a long day at school and hours of preparation for the next day, I had little enthusiasm to sit down and slog away at the mountain of work ahead of me, especially when it was over ninety degrees at midnight. Yet once I opened the package containing films of the masses I found in Dresden, my curiosity overcame my fatigue, and I dove into the project.

Almost daily, mail arrived with more microfilms. My first task was to make an overview of the manuscripts, forty-three in all by the time the last package arrived. I had microfilms from Dresden, Vienna, the monasteries I visited, and ten other libraries I had written to. Copies of Hasse's works came from all over Europe, another testimony to his importance as a composer.

Although having the microfilm reader at home was invaluable and no doubt saved my marriage, the films were negatives and presented another challenge. The hours looking at the white notation on a black background were harder on my yes than I realized. Often after a midnight session, I complained of numbing headaches. Something had to be done, or I feared I would go blind.

In order to maximize my time and extract as much information as possible, I made a list of questions to pose to each manuscript examined. I noted the title, movement, key, meter, length, form, vocal and instrumental forces, text, writing style, harmonic structure, musical motives, unusual features and condition of each manuscript. The result of this initial inquiry proved invaluable when I started writing, for I had more information about Hasse and his music than any other scholar had amassed, truly groundbreaking work.

Besides commenting on his music, I also intended to make a modern performance edition of two major works, so I was on the lookout for scores which looked interesting from a performance standpoint. The initial investigation proved fruitful. Two works stood out from all the rest: *Mass in D minor* (1751) and *Requiem in C major* (1763), works I knew were of particular importance to Hasse and the Dresden court.

After selecting these works as the main thrust of the study, I needed to find an easier way to work with them. The hours necessary to transcribe hundreds of pages of 18th century handwritten music into modern notation would prove to be more than daunting if I had to depend on the microfilm reader as my source for viewing the films.

A trip back to the media center solved the problem. They developed the films and made positive photocopies. I no longer needed the micro-film reader. I could jot down remarks in the margins of the pages and organize the immense task of transcribing tens of thousands of often illegible notes into smaller manageable segments. Breaking the project down this way made the task less Herculean, at least that is what I told myself.

What did I have to do to turn an 18th century score into a modern performance edition? The first challenge was reading the hand of the copyist who often used abbreviations and shorthand to complete his work. Having just examined dozens of manuscripts in Dresden and Vienna, I was somewhat familiar with the notation. The most laborious task, after deciphering the notes, was creating the orchestral score. Each page of a full score is comprised of lines and lines of music, one for each instrument or voice (choral or solo). In some cases this amounted to sixteen separate lines per page. I guessed from a quick glance at the scores, the Mass was about forty-five minutes long, and the Requiem almost an hour, a lot of music to hand copy into a full score. I felt numb at the prospect.

Next, was the complicated task of negotiating the various clefs 18th century musicians read. Unlike modern notation, where the majority of instruments and voices are written in treble or bass clef, 18th century musicians read as many as five different clefs to avoid adding ledger lines, lines which indicate a note above or below the staff. Not mixing up the clefs was another obstacle.

Technically speaking, sopranos read soprano clef, not the modern treble clef. The bottom line of the staff was not an E as we all learned as kids (EGBDF), but in Hassle's time was a C. Thus for a soprano the lines on the staff would be CEGBD. This school of notation, called "moveable clef," was the dominate system used by composers until the turn of the 20th century. I had studied the moveable clef system in music theory classes, but never became proficient. Until now, I had no need to, other than to pass a test. Now mastering these clefs became a necessity, and added one more hurdle to the project.

The third most difficult task was deciphering the figured bass line, the musical shorthand which dictated the harmonic progression of the work and told the keyboardist how to "realize" or play the accompaniment. These tiny numbers beneath the bass line were difficult to read and often inaccurate. I lost a lot of time solving mistakes which had to be notated in the dissertation appendix. An additional challenge was the text, which was often abbreviated or omitted.

Bringing an ancient piece of music to life was not easy, but I had to complete this part of the project before I could begin writing. So, night after night, like a monk in a monastery, I slugged away. Because of the complexity of the score, some pages took hours to transcribe, and I grew weary of writing down endless strings of 16th notes. Other pages were less complicated. As I became more proficient and facile with the clefs and handwriting, I started to see progress.

At first, I began transcribing the music using the kind of pen and ink required in composition classes. Then I realized here was a disaster waiting to happen. If I spilled ink or made a mistake, it would take hours to rectify. I would have to start all over again. I switched from ink to pencil and hoped my committee would accept the modification. After a quick call, my advisor assured me they would. Upon hearing this good news, I breathed a sigh of relief which I was sure could be heard blocks away.

To relieve the monotony of staring at the music, I organized the Vienna notes, and a picture of my mysterious composer came into focus. He was every bit the man I thought him to be. As I filled pages of legal sized paper with information, I felt him come to life. I now had in my possession more facts and examples of his music than anyone in recent history had gathered. Not even Dr. Novak or Dr. Reich had access to the rich musical library I had assembled. I was treading on virgin territory and looking at music that had lain dormant for hundreds of years.

I was on a mission and felt a great responsibility. If I didn't complete this work, who would? Just thinking about the ramifications gave me chills. I vowed to take my work seriously, as seriously as a scientist about to make a great discovery. For I felt I was doing just that, about to rediscover an 18th century musical genius.

Chapter Nineteen: Pulling Back the Veil

Who was this mysterious Mr. Hasse? What did I know about him? The picture emerging was a successful man, musician, composer, and diplomat hailed all over Europe. His creative life encompassed the entire 18th century. He had contact with the most important musicians of his day. His music, which spanned the High Baroque of Bach and Handel and the Classic period of Haydn and Mozart, served as a bridge between these two monumental epochs of music. But to quote the article in *Grove's Dictionary of Music and Musicians* which launched me on this project, his legacy was in doubt.

Hasse's facility in composition was astonishing. His career was one long success; few composers have enjoyed during their lifetime such world-wide celebrity as he; of those few none is more completely forgotten now.

The last line resonated in me. In Dresden I had experienced first-hand the truth of that statement, and I could feel myself being drawn into the middle of this enigma. How could someone so lauded, simply vanish?

To begin unraveling the mystery I made a list of the facts I knew.

Johann was born in the small village of Bergedorf near Hamburg on March 23, 1699 into a family of church musicians and organists. Petrus Hasse, his great grandfather, was organist in Lübeck, his son Friedrich in Salzwedel, and his son Peter, Hasse's father, in Bergedorf. The young Johann, raised in such a musical family, demonstrated talent as a singer. At age fifteen he was sent to Hamburg to study voice and composition. Three years later, he became a member of the opera company and subsequently was appointed composer and singer for the court of the von Braunscheigs, a wealthy family with strong connections to the Prince of

Saxony. By the age of twenty-one he had written his first opera, *Antioco*, which was a great success.

At the encouragement of his patron, Hasse was urged to study Italian opera, the style in vogue in all the European courts. Like the young Handel before him and many composers after, Hasse set out for Italy. For three years he traveled, observing musical life in Venice, Bologna, Florence, and Rome, before taking residence in Naples, one of the most musically eclectic cities of its day. In Naples, Hasse studied with Niccolo Porpora and Alessandro Scarlatti, two important teachers who introduced him to the vibrant church music scene.

Known all over Europe for their extravagant feast days, Neapolitan churches annually sponsored concerts and masses to honor their patron saints. A group of influential leaders, known as the Arcadian Academy, guided these festivals. Composed of popes, cardinals, bishops, local and foreign counts, artists, musicians, and wealthy devout patrons, the Academy recognized Hasse's talents and commissioned several operas, which were immediately acclaimed.

With his operatic successes and the blessings of the Academy, Hasse moved to Venice in 1727 where he was appointed *Kapellmeister* (head composer) of the *Conservatorium degli' Incurabili*, one of four prominent conservatories in Venice. Originally built as orphanages for young girls, in reality, the conservatories were schools of music which trained singers and instrumentalists. As their reputation grew, the orphanages attracted promising composers to write for their ensembles. Hasse wrote his *Miserere in C minor* (Psalm 51) for women's chorus and strings, the piece which started me on this quest, for this orphanage.

At a grand Venetian ball, Hasse met the enchanting operatic diva Faustina Bordoni, lauded as "a mezzo who could sing with a clarity and velocity which astonished all who heard her." I can image the handsome young Hasse in a red velvet tunic, his white-wigged ponytail tied with a black ribbon, gazing across the room at the woman who would soon become his wife. Faustina's suitors described her as "a beauty who could capture the heart of any man with her radiant smile and glorious voice." Hasse was so smitten, he wrote an opera for her. After a whirl-wind courtship, the two were wed.

The fame of the young German, who had operatic triumphs in Naples and now Venice, reached his homeland. In 1731, Hasse and his new wife were summoned to Dresden where he was named Royal Polish and Saxon *Kapellmeister*. As his first duty, he wrote an opera in the Italian style, trained the cast and directed the performances. Faustina sang the leading role. The resulting opera, *Cleofide*, was a resounding success. Repeated performances were immediately scheduled to satisfy the throngs wanting to hear this dazzling young star sing her husband's virtuosic music. Over night, the Hasses became the darlings of Dresden.

Hasse's fame spread. His operas were mounted all over Europe. A local critic wrote:

"This extraordinary couple can probably pass as the greatest virtuosos in music at the present time, for there is no equal of Herr Hasse in composition, nor of the incomparable Madame Hasse in singing and acting."

Johann and Faustina were magnificently received at the Dresden court of Friedrich August the Strong, King of Poland and Saxony. He earned his nickname by his sheer brute strength. It was said he could break horseshoes with his bare hands and liked to engage in the art of fox tossing. But his relationship with Hasse was short lived. In 1733, the King died while vacationing at his summer palace in Warsaw.

Fortunately for Hasse, the successor to the throne was Friedrich August the Third, whose love of the arts was even more passionate than his father's. Under the young Friedrich's leadership, Dresden became the musical center of Germany, and Johann and Faustina were the locus of that center.

Because of an unusual arrangement made with the King, Hasse did not have to accompany the court when they vacationed in Warsaw, often for extended periods of time. This agreement proved fortunate for the couple. It allowed them an opportunity to travel and revisit their beloved Italy. Hasse, therefore, led a double life, one as court appointed composer with a prescribed scope of duties, the other as a free-lance musician who was free to accept operatic engagements from other royal courts. No other composer of his day had such an arrangement, and Hasse took full advantage of it.

Now the story becomes more interesting. Seated in the audience at the first performance of *Cleofide* was none other than Johann Sebastian

Bach. He had been invited by the royal court to give an organ recital the next day. Hasse and Faustina, now considered distinguished members of the court, undoubtedly heard Bach's performance. They may have even met, for both were well aware of each other.

Hasse, on one hand, represented what is new in music, while Bach by then was considered old fashioned and stuffy; the young genius hailed for arias which could melt hearts, face to face with the "Father of the Fugue," the ancient art of creating complicated compositions requiring a learned approach to comprehend.

One of the courtiers was heard to remark upon leaving Bach's recital, "too many notes and way too loud." That opinion was shared by others, for Bach was seldom invited back to perform. He did, however, visit Dresden often to attend Hasse's opera performances. Hasse also ventured to Leipzig frequently, for he admired Bach's keyboard and improvisation skills.

Recognizing a new regime was in power, in 1733 Bach tried to seize upon this unique opportunity by making another visit to the Dresden court, this time not to play, but to apply for a position. He was growing tired of the pedantic tastes of Leipzig, and longed to end his relationship with the school at St. Thomas Church, where he was forced to teach Latin and music to unruly pupils. Lured by the successes of Hasse and his skilled ensembles, Bach sought the position of court composer.

To demonstrate his compositional skills, Bach submitted a "Kyrie" and "Gloria," the first two movements of the mass to showcase his prodigious talent. Comprised of twelve separate movements, one for each portion of text of the mass, each featured a different facet of Bach's genius. Several movements were written in the old contrapuntal style, others in the championed new style, which favored deftly crafted melodies and richer harmonies. Bach scored his audition piece for chorus, orchestra, two sopranos, tenor and bass. I can only conjecture that Bach wrote the second soprano part for Faustina, the reigning diva of her day. The dazzling duet for solo violin and mezzo soprano, the "Laudamus Te," is an example of an aria with soaring vocal lines and brilliant runs perfectly suited to her voice.

Was Bach trying to capture Hasse's favor by writing a movement specifically tailored for his wife? One which matched the color and agility critics raved about? A coincidence? I think not, but as yet I don't have evidence to prove it. Bach was a smart man and a diplomat. It seems logical he would try to win Hasse's approval by writing music for Faustina.

But Bach failed to impress the members of the court, who felt his style too old fashioned. Dejected, he left Dresden without the position. However, the music he wrote for the audition was not lost. At the end of his life, Bach returned to the work and completed what became his masterpiece, the *B minor Mass*, considered by the musical world as the crowning glory of the High Baroque.

For the court's musical ensembles, Hasse was given full rein to hire the finest instrumentalists and singers of the day. Many, like Hasse, were trained in Italy. With this confluence of talent, Dresden became the musical capital of Saxony. Far from appearing like a typical German city, the Dresden court thrived on importing the art and tastes of southern Europe. With his Italian training, Hasse found inspiration to fill the theater with grand opera and the royal church with magnificent mass settings.

Hasse's reputation in the world of music continued to grow. The new London Opera, the company in direct opposition to Handel's, invited Hasse in 1734 to the British capital. Not wanting to antagonize Handel, his fellow Saxon, Hasse refused. But that's not the whole story, for there is an amusing back story to this request.

Handel had previously engaged Faustina to sing in London. Her success was so impressive that the reigning prima donna, Francesca Cuzzoni, felt threatened and tried to stage a coup. Devastated that her young rival had more arias than she, Cuzzoni announced to Handel if he didn't write more music for her she would leap off the stage onto his harpsichord. Whereupon Handel is reputed to have replied, "Madame, pray tell me when you plan this feat, for far more will come to see you leap than hear you sing." Utterly humiliated, the diva stomped off stage. Faustina remained in London to finish the run of the production. She was now not only the sweetheart of Dresden and Venice, but of London as well.

With this amusing anecdote I found buried in an obscure German source, I was beginning to flesh out this famous pair. They were becoming real to me. Although I had hoped to uncover more about the Hasses, the lack of letters and communiqués was puzzling. Why couldn't

I find Hasse's personal correspondence? Where were his private notes and observations? One more piece of the puzzle yet to solve.

Hasse's interest in church music was first encouraged by Princess Maria Josepha, the wife of Augustus the Third. The daughter of Kaiser Joseph I of Austria, Maria's arrival in Dresden signaled a significant change. Augustus' court, which had been predominately Lutheran, was now officially Roman Catholic. For this new Catholic court Hasse created much of the church music I located.

Added to Hasse's growing reputation as an opera composer, he now became equally famous as a liturgical composer. European royalty sent their scribes to Dresden to make copies of Hasse's church music, as well as his operas. These handwritten copies enabled me to locate much of Hasse's forgotten church music. Had it not been for those scribes, I might have given up searching.

The two works I chose to edit, the *Mass in D minor* and the *Requiem in C*, were seminal to Hasse and his fame as a composer. Each played a significant role in his career and has a unique story to tell.

The mass was commissioned for the dedication of the *Hofkirche*, the new Catholic Church which Augustus the Third built as a present for his wife. From images I saw, it was an architectural gem. Designed in the high Baroque style, the church was nicknamed "the Wedding Cake," because of its exquisite exterior detail, but all I saw in Dresden was its bombed out ruins.

I could only imagine how glorious it must have been at the church's dedication on that warm summer Sunday morning in June of 1751. The entire court, and dignitaries from all over Europe, attended to honor Augustus and his wife. For this imperial occasion, Hasse wrote one of his most important works, the *Mass in D minor*. As the assembled guests arrived and the liturgical procession began, Hasse and his lauded court musicians from the rear organ loft began the opening strains of the stately "Kyrie." The resonant acoustics of the church, I am sure, caused all heads to turn and see where the glorious music was coming from. Although I have no evidence to support it, I am also certain that Faustina, who had just announced her retirement from the operatic stage, was one of the soloists. Her famous *bel canto* voice floating down from the balcony would have added much luster to the service. No wonder I found so many copies of this mass. The dedication of the *Hofkirche* was the musical event of the season. Composers and musicians flocked to Dresden to hear the music of the "divine Saxon" who was being lauded as the "Father of Music."

Among Hasse's many admirers, which included the French King Louis XV, and the Empress Maria Theresa of Austria, was Frederick II, King of Prussia, known as Frederick the Great. For Frederick, an amateur musician himself, Hasse wrote sixty flute sonatas and produced several operas in the King's palaces in Berlin and Potsdam. Their relationship, though cordial at first, soon turned tragic.

In order for Frederick to secure his Prussian holdings, his army invaded Saxony on their way to conquer Austrian occupied Silesia, a disputed land which lay to the southeast. The invasion was the beginning of the disastrous Seven Years' War, a conflict which soon involved the whole of Europe. To retaliate, the Austrians marched back through Saxony. With each invasion, Dresden was attacked. In 1760, near the end of the war, Frederick bombarded Dresden to keep it from falling into the hands of the enemy. Much of the city was destroyed, including the Royal Palace, the State Church and Hasse's private residence.

Along with his personal effects, all of Hasse's music, which was to be published as a collected edition by Brietkopf of Leipzig, perished. His life's work consumed by the flames. The Hasses, who had been touring Italy at the time, returned home to find their lives in ruin. With his home burned to the ground, his music destroyed, the royal court in shambles, and the coffers empty, Hasse's future looked bleak. But that's not the whole story. The total destruction of Dresden again, but this time by Allied Forces at the end of World War II, forever sealed the fate of Hasse and his legacy.

Had the promised royal edition been published by his patron, there is no doubt in my mind Hasse would be celebrated today as one of the great musical geniuses of his era. Like Bach and Handel, Hasse's name would have been known by all. Instead, his music perished in a fiery blaze, along with his letters and memorabilia. Although I was able to find copies of his most important scores, a great number of his works vanished altogether.

Years later, when the English historian Charles Burney visited Hasse in Vienna in 1772, he asked the now ailing composer for a list of his works. Hasse was obliged to admit he had forgotten most of them. He confessed to Burney, "like animals that procreate abundantly, he enjoyed the pleasure of producing his offspring more than preserving them." No one knows the extent of Hasse's output. Some musicologists conjecture he may have composed as many as sixty operas, a dozen oratorios, twenty masses, five requiems, ninety cantatas, numerous symphonies, concertos and hundreds of other works. He was indeed prolific.

Hasse's operas were visual and vocal spectacles written to dazzle and amaze the court. One theater critic described the 1755 production of the opera *Ezio* as a "sight the likes of which he had never seen."

It included eight thousand lamps and two hundred and fifty actors. The triumphal entry of Ezio alone took twenty-five minutes to pass by the stage, for it included four hundred soldiers, more than one hundred horses, five wagons, eight mules and a dozen camels. The closing ballet with three hundred dancers lasted forty-five minutes.

"The Age of Hasse" at the Dresden court shone brilliantly for almost thirty years (1731-1760), and cast its shadow all over Europe. Of the estimated sixty operas Hasse wrote for his patron, fifteen are thought to have starred Faustina. But the tide was soon to change.

With his residence destroyed, Dresden in ruins, and the Saxon King and his court fleeing to Warsaw, the Hasses gratefully accepted an invitation from the Empress Maria Theresa to join the Viennese court. She immediately commissioned an opera from her new "Maestro of Music" to honor the wedding of her son Joseph II.

An amateur musician herself, the Empress studied composition with Hasse. Although nothing significant came from her lessons, both student and teacher were happy with the arrangement. For Hasse, Maria's largesse allowed him to be a member of the most important court in Europe. Artists, musicians and poets flocked to Vienna to please the Empress, now the most influential woman of her day.

But again, the tide was soon to change. In Vienna, Hasse met the aspiring young composer Christoph Willibald Gluck. He espoused new ideas for the future of opera; ideas which soon would bury the success Hasse had so singularly enjoyed. No longer were complicated plots, casts of hundreds, elaborate scenery, and unapproachable characters in vogue. Under Gluck's reforms, simplicity and honesty became the focus.

155

Audiences now demanded an emotional connection with the plot, the music, and the libretto.

The "Age of Hasse" was over and he knew it. Hasse's fall was further solidified when he met the young prodigy Mozart. Recognizing Mozart's gifts, Hasse announced, "He will surely put us all in the shade." Unfortunately for Hasse, his prophecy became all too true.

Hasse did have one more connection with the Dresden court which was of significance. After the Peace of Hubertusberg (February 15, 1763), signaling the end of the Seven Years' War, Augustus and his court returned to Dresden after their long exile in Warsaw. For the celebration which was also the King's birthday, Hasse wrote a new opera. On the day of the dress rehearsal Augustus died of a stroke. His successor, Friedrich Christian, who was not disposed to Hasse or his music, nor obliged to empty his coffers for expensive court entertainment, dismissed Hasse without pension. However, out of gratitude to Augustus, Hasse composed the *Requiem in C major*, the score I chose to edit. Like the *Mass* he wrote for Maria Josepha, the *Requiem* was Hasse's personal paean to Augustus, his beloved patron. Hasse poured his heart and soul into it, and the *Requiem* was a resounding success, judging from the fact so many copies were found.

After the funeral, Hasse and Faustina left the now inhospitable Dresden and returned to Vienna and the warm welcome of the court of the Empress. Once again, he encountered the young Mozart, who now was fifteen. The Empress commissioned Hasse and Mozart each to compose an opera for the wedding of the Archduke Ferdinand. Hasse suffered from gout and had to dictate much of the score to his daughter. All accounts state Mozart's' opera was more impressive. Hasse's once renowned reputation suffered a fatal blow, and he was forced to retreat even further from the spotlight he once had singularly enjoyed.

The Hasses remained in Vienna until the spring of 1773 when they decided to return to their beloved Venice. Once settled, Hasse lived a secluded life, giving lessons and dedicating himself to the musical education of his two daughters, Peppina and Christina.

Hasse became embittered. Illness tormented him. He suffered financial loss when his bank closed. Death robbed him of his beloved Faustina, who died on November 4, 1781 at the age of eighty-one. Hasse followed her in death two years later on December 16, 1783. He was buried with little fanfare in the Church of San Marcuola in Venice. When news of his death reached Germany, few lamented. The Saxon, once the darling of Dresden and all of Europe, was forgotten. The fickle interests of the music world had already shifted to the new geniuses—Haydn and Mozart.

So ends the tragic story of Hasse, summed up by the 19th century historian Mennicke:

> . . . *in the entire history of music, there has never been another case like that of Hasse; no musician has ever been so popular as he was, none has won so quickly and completely the loudest recognition of both the musical experts and the music-loving public, and none was forgotten so quickly and unanimously.*

Chapter Twenty: Finishing?

At last, Hasse was on paper. I had discovered who he was, why he was forgotten, and why his music, along with his reputation, vanished into thin air. Most of the pieces of the puzzle, which had dogged me for so long, were in place. The picture emerging was clearer than ever. All that was left to complete the puzzle and come to grips with Hasse's talent was to reconstruct his music. I knew in order to accomplish this goal I had to transcribe the manuscripts by hand, which translated to hundreds of hours of work. In short, I had to become a scribe, like the ones the crown heads of Europe sent to Dresden to copy Hasse's music and bring it back to their court. In a way, I was doing the same thing.

So what did I know about his music? What had the fruits of my labor uncovered? To my astonishment, I had unearthed forty-three manuscripts. Ten European libraries contributed information and supplied microfilms. All the manuscripts were hand-copied. With the exception of the *Miserere*, no published scores were found. The only thing going for me was the memory of how smitten I was with that piece, and how I was hoping to find many more works equally satisfying. I had a tape of my original performance. Listening to it helped keep the sound of his music in my ear.

After sifting through all the evidence, I could say with some confidence that nine masses, several mass fragments and two requiems were composed by Hasse. This number was far more than I or anyone else thought existed. When I called my advisor and told him my results, he was amazed.

"Well, you certainly proved the committee wrong," he remarked with a hint of glee in his voice. "I bet you have more information about Hasse than anyone else has had for centuries."

"I couldn't have done it without your support," I responded, hoping he could hear the gratitude I felt for him. "Thanks for not giving up on me."

"Send me whatever you can, and I will guide you from here on. I can't wait to see the look on my colleagues' faces when I tell them of your progress." There was such a hint of pleasure in his voice; I knew I had won the battle.

With my advisor's complete blessing I plunged ahead. My plan was to finish editing the works and then begin writing. I estimated it would take four or five months to transcribe the music and another four or five months to complete the document. I saw no reason why I couldn't finish my dissertation in a year.

That was wishful thinking. As soon as I began teaching and conducting, my time and energy was consumed with planning rehearsals and preparing lectures. The work load for new professors was crushing. I had three choral ensembles to conduct, two academic classes to teach, and five private voice students. In addition to the teaching load, I was expected to visit local high schools and colleges, recruit singers and potential grad students, and attend faculty and committee meetings. By the time I got home, I was already exhausted. In addition, I was the director of a church music program, which meant weekly staff meetings, rehearsals and Sunday services. Just planning for all those responsibilities, let alone executing them, was a full time job.

But the little voice in my head and the louder one from my wife kept repeating "if you don't do it now, you will never finish." I knew how true those words were. Several of my colleagues at Illinois were in the same position. One had already given up. I was not a quitter, I told myself. I would find a way.

After trial and error, I developed a schedule which worked for me. Every night, Monday through Saturday, no matter what, I would stop what I was doing at ten o'clock and work on the dissertation. Just as in Genesis, I rested on the Sabbath, but not until conducting the music at two church services.

Some days were fruitful and others discouraging. Like Sisyphus, I often felt I was doing mind-numbing work, pushing a large stone up the mountain only to have it roll back again. Progress was slow. On nights I completed two or more measures of music, I considered it a triumph.

When I grew tired of writing notes on the page, I counted the measures in each movement to determine the length of the work. The Mass totaled nine hundred and fifteen! At the rate I was going, it would take me over a year to complete one manuscript. I estimated the Requiem was even longer. Was I looking at two years of work before I began writing? The thought was numbing.

Happily, I found the more I slugged away, the faster I became, and some nights I was able to complete ten or more measures. The longer I stared at the hand-written manuscript, the defter I became, and soon the work seemed to be purring along.

The music I began to hear in my head was even more engaging than I hoped. Hasse's lyric melodies, rich harmonies and colorful orchestrations, gave every evidence of the musical genius he was touted to be. He could write heart-wrenching arias and powerful choruses rivaling any found in Handel's oratorios. I could not wait to bring this stunning music to life, and that thought propelled me even more.

Night after night, week after week, month after month, I slaved away. When I put my pencil down after the last "Amen," it was the middle of May, nine months after I started. I was so far behind schedule, I called my advisor.

"Dr. Hamm, I have a critical question to ask. I finished editing the Mass, but it took much longer than I planned. Do I still have to edit the Requiem?"

"Absolutely," was his reply, "or else you will have to resubmit to the committee. Do you want to face off with them again?"

He reminded me I proposed to edit two works, and two works is what I must do. I thanked him for his candor, put the phone down, and reluctantly picked up my pencil.

The Requiem project at first appeared even more daunting. The twenty-three separate movements added up to nine hundred and thirty-nine measures. Another nine months of work? I was numb. Yet once I had broken the code of the notation, I found it easier to edit; the manuscript was clearer, the writing less complicated. The work moved along quicker.

Choosing not to teach summer school, I used the extra time to triple my work load, hoping to finish the Requiem transcription by the end of August. This decision turned out to be the right one. We were expecting our first child in the fall, and I knew I had to pitch in more around the house. Other than church duties and Lamaze child birth classes, my summer months were devoted to Mr. Hasse.

When I thought all was going well, I received a letter from the University which shook me to the core. Short and concise, it stated my appointment would not be renewed. As of August 15th I would be terminated. No reasons were given, just the cold facts. Signed "Sincerely," Dean of the School of Music, I seethed inside as I read the fateful words.

Devastated and shaking, I handed the letter to my expectant wife. Her faced turned ashen when she read the shocking news. What was I going to do with a child on the way, a mortgage to pay, and no prospect of employment in sight?

My first thought was to fight, so I sought advice from colleagues who had been supportive of my work. They suggested I demand to know why I was being terminated and helped me craft a letter to the Dean and the University President. I also enlisted the help of the local chapter of the AAUP, the professional organization which handles academic matters.

Word leaked out of my termination and many of my colleagues and students wrote letters of support. When the Dean's response arrived, it was blunt. The music department was moving in another direction. I was not included in those plans.

As I later found out, I had ruffled his feathers which proved enough to terminate me. Internal politics played a major role. Decisions regarding the School of Music were not made by my Dean, but by his superior, the Dean of Fine Arts. He was a frustrated conductor who did not get a position he coveted and blamed me for getting in his way. He made the decision to fire me.

When it was clear whom I was dealing with, I went to the President of the University and poured out my heart to him. A scholar, well respected and newly appointed, he listened to my case. He seemed concerned. As it turned out, I had a lot going for me. Word had reached him of my predicament, and he was most sympathetic. He too was a graduate of the University of Illinois and knew personally of the superior reputation of the School of Music. He even had made some calls and talked to professors who knew of my work.

161

With a stack of supportive letters in his hand and a recommendation from the AAUP on his desk, he proposed the following solution. My nemesis was indeed the Dean of Fine Arts, a pretty big man to fight. If I agreed not to embroil the school in a lengthy and costly law suit, he would recommend I be granted one more year of employment, giving me time to finish the degree, apply for other positions, sell the house and move on.

Although still seething inside, I listened to his wise advice. By this time, all I could think of was revenge, not a good option. My anger was eating at me so much I found it difficult to function. I had to make a quick decision, so I accepted his offer. As he shook my hand, he added, I was young, had a great career ahead of me, and he would make sure my teaching load was reduced so I would have time to help my wife take care of our baby and finish the degree.

Years later, when I moved to much greener pastures, I learned the Dean of the School of Music had been sacked, and a year later so was the Dean of Fine Arts. In a way I did have my revenge, but just a little too late to allow me to stay at the U of A.

The summer months proved profitable. By the time school began in September, I had finished the *Requiem* score and was beginning to write the dreaded dissertation. If only I had a computer then, the project would have been so much easier. With no spell-check or way to move paragraphs around, the writing was tedious. It took days to craft the first sentence. The little voice in my head kept saying "it must be perfect or the committee will reject it." To say I often had writer's block was an understatement.

Where to begin? How to organize the boxes of notes and piles of music? I knew if I used my typewriter, I might have to spend hours erasing and crossing out words. I decided to employ the system I used in grad school—write in long hand on yellow-lined paper. This method of taking notes served me well; why abandon my proven method now. At least this way, I could cut and paste if I wanted to change the order of things.

Referring to my theses proposal which listed the chapter titles, I set out to write in that order.

With a little careful editing, I had already written Chapter One in Vienna, so I moved on to Chapter Two, a description of the manuscripts. By listing each one, its contents, its location, and its unusual features, this chapter practically wrote itself.

Chapter Three, which was dictated by the committee, was most challenging. Other than the music of Bach, few musicologists had explored 18th century church music in general and Neapolitan music in particular. In Hasse's case, no one had recently examined his masses. Most historians assumed they were written in a style similar to other opera composers of the day. I strongly disagreed and set out to prove it. My research proved Hasse had two styles, one for opera and one for church music.

Most helpful for my research on this chapter was the book Dr. Reich presented to me. It proved invaluable, and I thanked him often as I referred to it. The book contained a detailed account of Hasse's life at the Dresden court and valuable information about the Royal Church.

Chapter Four, "Stylistic Characteristics of Hasse's Masses," was the most satisfying to write. By posing the same questions to each of the forty-three manuscripts, this chapter represented the heart of my dissertation and was most original in terms of what I had uncovered.

With the mounds of information collected, fleshing out Hasse's musical style was not difficult. The research had proven so successful, I really understood this man and his music. My biggest challenge was finding the right language to document my findings. With the information contained in this chapter, I knew without a doubt I was making a significant contribution. I was breaking new ground and thumbing my nose at the naysayers.

During my second year at the university, things changed dramatically. Our son was born, grandparents had visited, and we were learning to adjust to a new schedule. With a lighter teaching load, I was able to be more helpful around the house, spend more time writing, and begin the laborious process of finding a new teaching position.

As most opportunities aren't advertised until spring, there were few I could apply for. But I inquired to any school which looked promising. I needed to get my name out there, and fast.

The most promising lead was not from professional journals or colleagues, but from a new acquaintance. My wife's reputation as a fine violinist landed her a job in the Tucson Symphony, the only professional gig in town. At a party given by the conductor, I met a visiting musician hired to play contrabassoon on the concert. While chatting with him for a few minutes, I learned two valuable facts: he was a professor at Portland State University and the school was looking for a choral conductor. I jumped at the chance to apply and immediately sent off a letter of introduction to the search committee. After several letters and phone calls, I was invited to interview. An appointment was set for the last week in November.

The interview went well, better than I had hoped. The students were eager, the faculty cordial, and I fell in love with the area. Portland was the antitheses of Tucson—vibrant, green, youthful, as opposed to old, staid and desolate. As I stepped off the plane back in Tucson and embraced my wife, I felt the job was in my pocket. No more worries.

But was I too optimistic?

After not hearing a word in weeks, I received a letter from the Dean stating they had to delay the decision. The department was facing financial problems. They were not sure they would fill the position at this time.

My heart sank when I read the news. Hopes dashed, my prospects looked glum. I resumed applying. I had no other choice.

Well into the spring semester when I still didn't have any solid leads, I began to panic. The writing was going well, but what good would the degree do if I were still unemployed. If I couldn't get a job soon, what would we do? Sell the house? Move? But where?

164

If you believe the old adage, "when one door closes another one opens," I am living proof it is true.

Late one afternoon, as I was sitting at my desk grading papers and feeling sorry for myself, my wife called. Portland State wanted to talk with me at my earliest convenience. Well my earliest convenience was now, so I nervously dialed the number and waited.

The secretary answered and put me through to the Dean. He began by saying, "It gives me great pleasure to tell you as the unanimous choice of the search committee, we would like to offer you the position of Director of Choral and Vocal Studies at Portland State."

I was so excited by the news I didn't hear the "but." The "but" was the position would be half-time for the first year, and then convert to a full-time tenure tract the following year.

When I processed what he said, I impertinently asked, "Instead of starting in September on a half-time appointment, could I begin in January on a full-time one?"

After a long pause he said, "Yes, I think we can make that work. I'll send you a contract with all the details. Plan to be in Portland by the first week of January for orientation."

I hoped he heard the relief and gratitude in my voice, as I thanked him for his support and faith in me. I was so overwhelmed, I forgot to ask him about the salary.

No sooner had I placed the phone back on the receiver when it rang again. Assuming it was my wife anxious to know our fate I blurted out the good news.

A stunned silence followed. I imagined she was jumping up and down with glee, but instead she said in a hushed voice, "Are you sitting down?" Why the mystery? Was she OK? Was the baby sick? I couldn't imagine what was wrong or why she was calling back so soon.

"We just got an offer on our house," she said, her voice at such a high pitch I had difficulty understanding her. "And from the first couple who viewed it this morning!"

"What did you say?" I shouted, my voice now rising to a pitch similar to hers.

"But honey, that's not all." She was so excited she could barely speak. "They offered us our full asking price, not just for the house, but for the land as well."

At the wise suggestion of our realtor we divided up the offer. We listed the house apart from the adjoining four acres. At first I was skeptical, but later agreed. What did we have to lose? If we only sold the house, we would at least break even.

In the space of several minutes our prayers were answered. I had a new job; we sold our property and doubled our money. In less than two years our over-priced home had given back to us two-fold.

"Get a baby sitter, Honey. We're going to celebrate tonight!"

Chapter Twenty-One: Really Finishing

News of our good fortune spread. The next weekend close friends and colleagues held a party to celebrate and wish us well. Conspicuously missing from the festive gathering were the Deans. Rumors circulated because of the way they botched my case, their time was limited. I hoped they were busy licking their wounds knowing it was a matter of time before they would receive their walking papers. Several old-timers whispered to me they wanted to leave the university too, but with tenure and a home free and clear, it made no sense.

Several days later I received a note from the President congratulating me on my new appointment and wishing me all the best. I was touched and called him. He had given me such good advice I wanted him to know how grateful I was. Although I would miss the university, I was eager to press on as he wisely suggested.

With that call I closed the book on one the most painful chapters of my young life. Being fired from my first college job was not the way I wanted to start my career. But I knew from such an inauspicious start, better times had to be ahead for me and my family.

With the home sold and a new job waiting for me in January, I thought about our next move. What should we do? Ship the furniture to San Jose and stay with my wife's parents? Rent a house in Tucson, get a part-time job doing anything and wait the time out, or do something daring?

At my wife's urging we chose the latter. As soon as I finished the degree, she proposed we visit her sister in London, and then spend the rest of the year in Vienna. How could I not love such a dreamer?

If she was willing to take the gamble, so would I. No better place to lick my wounds than Vienna!

The next two months were a whirlwind of activity. In between teaching, getting ready for the move, and making arrangements to live in Vienna, I managed to squeeze in enough time to finish the writing just as the movers arrived to pack up our things. I think the last item to go into the truck was my typewriter.

I called my advisor and we discussed what had to be done to prepare for the defense; it was numbing. The list was longer than I thought. I would have to be on campus for several weeks to complete all the requirements.

First, he had to approve the writing. Then he dropped a bombshell. He admitted he hadn't had time to read any of the chapters I sent him. He hadn't read a word? What if he rejected what I wrote? Would I have to start all over? I was paralyzed.

He assured me as soon as I arrived on campus we would have ample time go over each chapter, make any changes, and then submit a copy to the committee. After they read and approved the final draft, it would be submitted to the graduate school for document approval. Upon scaling those hurdles, the formal defense would be scheduled.

Assuming I passed, he suggested I hire a professional thesis typist to prepare the final copies which in turn are sent to the university bindery. Although the list was long, at least I could see light at the end of the tunnel. Soon, I could say in spite of all the obstacles and years of work, "I did it!"

With my wife and baby in San Jose and the furniture stored, I clutched the box containing the completed dissertation in my hand and boarded the plane for the flight to Chicago and then on to Urbana. No way was I going to let it out of my sight. I had heard horror stories of theses burning in fires, disappearing in lost luggage, or vanishing in the mail. I wasn't going to take any chances. My friend who lived in 'tornado alley' told me he kept his dissertation in the freezer for safekeeping.

Being back on the campus felt like homecoming. Although it was still hot and muggy, I didn't care. I had come full circle.

The meeting with my advisor went well. He gave me excellent suggestions on how to organize the material to make it more readable. I made the changes, submitted the corrected copies to the committee members, and waited.

Days later the call came and I set the date for the formal defense. When I entered the familiar conference room I thought my knees would buckle. The same fear I felt at my oral exam gripped me, for I knew my fate was in the hands of those waiting for me.

For two hours I championed my composer and his music before the very ones who doubted my topic. With score in hand I pointed out Hasse's musical characteristics, his melodic genius, his harmonic inventiveness, and his rich orchestrations. Several nodded in approval while others sat stony-faced. I was getting mixed messages. What would their verdict be?

Finally, the questions stopped. I was ushered out of the room. I paced up and down the hall as they debated my fate. Each tick of the clock on the wall sounded like a death knell.

The door opened. I saw smiles on their faces. I knew I had passed. Shaking my hand and calling me "Doctor" for the first time, they told me how impressed they were with my research. I had written a new chapter in the history of church music. Even the naysayers said they couldn't believe how much music I had found, music they were convinced no longer existed.

"Let's go to the Faculty Club and have a drink to celebrate," Dr. Decker, my mentor and major professor suggested.

"Please let me call my wife in San Jose first," I countered with tears of joy rolling down my cheeks.

Dialing the number, I couldn't contain myself.

"Honey, I passed," I blurted out, and the rest I don't remember. I do recall saying something like, "You don't have to call me 'Doctor' but you can if you like."

The noise coming from the other end of the line told me glasses were clinking as the news spread to the rest of the family gathered in the living room. The completion of this degree was a milestone, not just for me, but for the whole family. I was not the first to finish college or go to graduate school, but the first to receive a doctorate.

I was proud of my accomplishment, but much more grateful for the support I received from my mentors and those who believed in me, mostly my wife who sacrificed so much to make this dream come true. As a symbol of my thankfulness I dedicated the dissertation to her and to my parents.

I will never forget the feeling I had stepping off the plane with degree in hand on that summer day in June knowing all my formal education was behind me. But I also knew it was just the beginning. Grad school had given me the tools, now I had to learn to apply them.

❧   ❧   ❧

Two weeks later we arrived in London on the hottest day in recent history. With sweat dripping and loaded down with luggage, stroller, and diaper bags, we moved into the small upstairs apartment of my wife's sister.

After a week of adjusting to our new sense of freedom, we flew to Amsterdam and picked up our fire-engine red Fiat station wagon which would be our home for the duration of the trip. Driving through France and Switzerland on our way to Austria, staying in quaint little villages, shopping every day for food and diapers, visiting churches and museum with our eight-month-old son on my back, are memories I will treasure forever.

Arriving in Vienna, we felt the magic and majesty of the city we both loved return, and took full advantage of our good fortune. We went to operas, concerts and plays. I again sang with the Choir of St. Augustine, Camilla joined the Vienna Academy Orchestra. We skied in the Austrian Alps, hiked in the Vienna Woods, celebrated our son's first birthday at Demel's, took carriage rides around the *Stephensdom*, visited our favorite museums, sailed down the Danube, and ventured out into villages surrounding the city. And yes, I personally delivered a copy of my dissertation to Dr. Nowak, who noticing his name in the acknowledgments, smiled.

The night before we left to return home, Camilla played a concert in the *Musikverien*, the home of the Vienna Philharmonic. Busting with pride, I sat in that famed hall and watched my beloved wife add the final "note" to our adventure.

We said a tearful goodbye to our temporary home and flew back to the States to spend the holidays with family before moving up to Portland to begin the next phase of our life.

The adventures we experienced during those six months in Europe defined our family. We were risk-takers, explorers. Never the safe way.

No, not for us. We proved we could gamble and come out ahead. Now what lay ahead?

સ્ર સ્ર સ્ર

Like the Hasses in Dresden, we were warmly welcomed in Portland where we quickly made new friends and became involved in the vibrant musical life of the city. I conducted three choirs at the university, taught choral conducting and music education classes, and was director of the symphony chorus. Cami taught strings in the local schools, had a studio of budding young violinists, and played in several orchestras. Life was good!

Years passed before I thought of Hasse again. After spending so much time and energy researching, and hundreds of hours writing, I was not anxious to revisit the topic. Life in all its complexities completely engulfed me. Teaching, rehearsing and conducting consumed all of my energy. I was either giving a lecture or planning one; conducting a concert or planning the next one. Time flew by.

After four years in Portland, I was offered a wonderful opportunity. The University of Southern California had an opening in their renowned choral department. Naturally, I applied and was more than surprised when the call came that I had been chosen. Again we said tearful goodbyes, packed up a twenty-four foot U-haul truck and made the difficult move to Los Angeles.

Life in the big city was even more hectic than in Portland. Besides a full-time tenure tract position and directing the music at a big downtown church, I became artistic director of the Camerata Singers and the Long Beach Bach Festival. As in Portland, Cami taught strings in the local schools, developed a studio of private violin students and played in several very active orchestras. Our second son was born and every moment seemed to be filled.

Would I ever find time to do anything with my Hasse scores? I doubted it. I was too busy with school, church, the Bach Festival and family.

But the thought I had yet to produce any of Hasse's music ate at me. I looked for ways to bring his scores to life. As the year 1983 approached, marking the 200th anniversary of Hasse's death, I thought about

171

mounting some kind of festival in Dresden to honor the event and bring attention to him and his music.

I contacted the German Embassy in San Francisco for advice. They gave me several names to write to at the East German Consulate in Berlin. After many attempts and no response, I gave up on the idea. There was no interest in the project, and obviously no interest in cooperating with anyone from the West.

Several years later I read that East German musicologists were going to publish Hasse's complete works. I sent a letter of inquiry to the publisher in Dresden to see if I could submit my editions. This time at least I received a response. "Only East German scholars could contribute to the project."

The break for me came on November 9, 1989 when the miracle no one thought possible became a reality.

The wall came down!

After years of occupation, the Brandenburg gates opened, thousands crossed, families were united, and the healing of ruptured Berlin began. I contacted the German Embassy again, but was told even though the city was re-opened, Russian authorities were still in command. I would have to work with the East German government in Dresden. After many attempts and no reply, I put the idea aside for the second time.

June, 1994—Russian troops reluctantly filed out of Germany. They dreaded going back to the bleak existence awaiting them in their corrupt homeland. Could I resurrect the project now that the political climate had changed so dramatically? My new target date for the festival would be 1999, the 300th anniversary of Hasse's birth. I was certain I could create some interest in Dresden for such an important cultural event, and I had five years to plan it.

Instead of trying to contact the Embassy, I wrote to the director of the *Hochschule für Musik*, the most important school of music in Dresden. Would they be interested in co-sponsoring a festival dedicated to one of their most famous musicians?

The response I received was curt and to the point. The director first admitted he had little knowledge of Hasse, and then added any festival mounted in Dresden would have to be under the auspices of the Saxon Arts Council. I replied I was eager to cooperate in any way. I just wanted to complete my now thirty year quest to conduct Hasse's music in the city which made him famous; more specifically, to conduct my edition of Hasse's *Mass in D minor* in the *Hofkirche*, the church where it was premiered in 1751.

The next response was even more abrupt: "The church was destroyed in World War II and still lays in ruins; there is no way a concert could be performed there."

My heart sank as I read those words. I could feel my dream slipping through my fingers. Although I believed in the adage "the third time is a charm," my third attempt was an abject failure. How could I make my dream possible with no interest or support?

Chapter Twenty-Two: Retribution

"Where there is a will there is a way," my father's words echoed in my ear. I definitely had the will; now I had to find the way. There had to be something I could do to fulfill the dream now burning even brighter inside me. But what?

I approached the Board of the Camerata Singers, the choir I had been conducting for the past ten years, with a plan I hoped they would approve. They had long been tossing around the idea of a concert tour to either China, where we had a long standing invitation, or to Brazil, where as a visiting professor at the Sacred Music Institute in Campinas, I had many contacts. The declining political climate in Beijing shut the first idea down, and the skyrocketing inflation in Brazil convinced some board members that the venture was too risky. Conservative wisdom prevailed. The idea of a tour was dropped.

The plan I proposed was more specific—concerts in Vienna, Prague, Leipzig, Dresden and Berlin. My goal was still the same, "Hasse in Dresden." But why not add another wrinkle, "Bach in Leipzig." The Camerata Singers, noted for producing the annual Long Beach Bach Festival, had performed all of Bach's major works. Hasse spent thirty years in Dresden. Bach the same amount of time in Leipzig. Why not perform both composers' music on the tour, after all, in real life their lives often intertwined. The Board embraced the idea and appointed a committee to work with me on the plans.

Since there is no shortage of companies organizing concert tours, I contacted ones with the best reputation and invited them to submit bids. The requirements for the tour were: a maximum of 16 days, price to include air fare, ground transportation, city tours, hotels, some meals, and a minimum of five concerts. I estimated with forty singers, an orchestra of twenty-two, plus spouses and friends, a total of about seventy, we would need two large buses to have room for instruments, music stands and choral risers.

The tour was beginning to resemble the one I took in 1969 with the Santa Clara Chorale. For the one hundred and fifteen member entourage on that tour, we hired four buses. On our way to Vienna, one broke down and we had to pile people, luggage and instruments onto the other buses. What a nightmare. I didn't want to repeat that experience again. I was hoping for creative solutions.

At the next rehearsal, I made the pitch to the choir to see what their reaction would be. They were more than enthusiastic and soon I had commitments from half the singers. The remaining wanted to wait until they had a clearer picture of the costs. I could not blame them. I too was curious to know what we were getting ourselves into.

Several weeks later, the bids came in. One proposal in particular piqued my interest. Instead of contracting an orchestra from the States, which would entail substantial underwriting in order for the players to sign on, it was suggested we could hire an orchestra in Germany for a lot less. If we limited the orchestral concerts to two, Leipzig and Dresden, and performed the other concerts with organ, we could eliminate the expense of the orchestra traveling with us. The idea made sense to me and to the Board.

The next challenge was finding an orchestra which suited our needs and budget. Again the winning bidder came through with the perfect solution—the *Pauliner Barockensemble, Leipzig*, an orchestra specializing in Bach and 18th century music.

I contacted their director, and we began corresponding. As the orchestra is based in Leipzig, site of the first concert, he proposed they drive to Dresden for the second one. The trip would take about an hour and a half. After the concert, they would drive back home. This plan would eliminate two major expenses—lodging and transportation. What a brilliant idea!

When the revised proposal came back from the tour company with the new figures I knew it was a "go." By hiring an orchestra instead of taking one, the costs dropped and the Board signed on. With the details of the tour now finalized, I presented the plan to the choir. We would leave Los Angeles on June 17, 1999 and return July 1. In Vienna, Prague, Nymburk and Berlin we would sing with organ accompaniment, and in Leipzig and Dresden we would perform the Hasse and Bach works with the *Pauliner Orchestra*. The response was overwhelming. When I told them the total individual cost, all forty singers signed on.

My next challenge was to physically produce the music. The Bach parts would not be a problem. I could purchase them from the publisher. But what about the Hasse work? Although I had completed the full score of the Mass, I was by no means finished with the editing project. In order to perform the work, I had to make instrumental and choral parts. Another massive project stared me in the face. I counted the measures and estimated it would take hundreds of hours to write out the parts. With no budget to hire copyists, I had to do the work myself, a project I dreaded even thinking about. I was way too busy with school, church, concerts, and family to find time for this extra chore. There must be another way to solve the problem.

I stewed about my dilemma for days. How to solve this perplexing yet important problem? As I was about to sit down and begin copying, a crazy idea came to me. Why not photocopy the score then cut and paste the parts together? It would be labor intensive, but a lot faster and more accurate than re-writing the parts by hand.

The next day I put my plan to the test. Starting with the winds, then strings, soloists, chorus and lastly the keyboard, I cut up a copy of my handwritten score and created all the parts. I sent them off to the *Pauliner Orchestra* and held my breath. Would my plan work? Had I solved the problem? Could they use my reconstructed parts? "Yes," was the director's answer. I breathed a sigh of relief. All was now in place.

Our tour of a lifetime was now less than a year away. I had plenty of time to develop a strategy. Since my goal was to perform the music for the tour well in advance, I planned the entire 1998-1999 season accordingly. There would be no last minute frantic rehearsals for this tour. No, not like others I had taken.

The repertoire I chose to perform with the orchestra would be Hasse's *Mass* and a magnificent cantata Bach often performed in Leipzig —Cantata 21, *Ich hatte viel Bekümmernnis* (I had much affliction). This impressive work featured a prominent role for both chorus and soloists, and would be the perfect pairing with the Hasse work.

For the other concerts (Vienna, Prague, Nymburk and Berlin), I relied on the talents of my colleagues at USC. Morten Lauridsen, Chair of the Theory and Composition Department and a close personal friend, had just written a work titled *Lux Aeterna*, a composition for chorus and organ which was receiving critical acclaim. A hauntingly beautiful work based on Latin texts embodying the word "light," it would be perfect for the acoustics of the cavernous cathedrals we would sing in. When I approached the composer with the idea, he graciously gave me permission to give the European premiere. I was honored and humbled by his confidence in me and the Camerata. Another colleague, James Hopkins, a renowned organist and composer, contributed two other impressive pieces.

For the rest of the program, I chose music which held a special place in my heart. None fit the description better than Randall Thompson's perfectly crafted *Alleluia*, the signature piece of my mentor J. Russell Bodley, Dean of the Conservatory of Music at the College of the Pacific. He was the first to give me an opportunity to conduct and was a constant source of inspiration and encouragement. Under his guidance, I received both my bachelor's and master's degrees. As conductor of Pacific's famed A Cappella Choir, he often included this eloquent and moving paean to peace on concerts we performed. He championed me, and by my programming this piece on the tour I found a way to honor him.

I will never forget the first time I sang the *Alleluia*. The choir was standing on an island in the middle of Mirror Lake in Yosemite Valley on a chilly Easter morning, fog rising from the waters surrounding us. As the sun majestically rose over Half Dome, shooting golden rays of light across the lake, we sang this inspired work.

Just thinking about that transforming moment brings tears to my eyes. Several years later, during that magical summer at Tanglewood which changed my life, I sang it again, this time with the composer conducting. Such were the memories buried deep within, and I wanted them to be a part of this very special tour.

I also programmed another work by Thompson, *The Last Words of David*, which had a virtuoso organ part and was a favorite of my choirs. I balanced personal choices with academic ones: Renaissance motets by Palestrina, Weelkes, Byrd, di Lasso and Gibbons, all composers I had written significant research papers on at the U of I. I remember feeling so proud when I received an A+ on the Byrd paper from Dr. Ringer, the brilliant yet most demanding musicologist on the faculty.

The eclectic program, which I hoped would engage the audience and inspire the choir, was still not complete. Having toured many times before, I knew European audiences loved hearing American folksongs and spirituals, so I included several of my favorites. With the program set, at least on paper, I was one step closer to the goal

℞ ℞ ℞

The master plan worked. We sang the Bach Cantata on the October concert, and after the holidays, began rehearsing the rest of the music for the tour.

With eager excitement, I handed out the chorus parts to the Hasse Mass at the first rehearsal of the New Year. Something was in the air. I could feel it. We all could feel it. We were about to make musical history.

The choir sat up straight with score in hand and awaited the magical moment. You could have heard a pin drop when I raised my arms and cued the accompanist. As the choir listened to the opening measures, the anticipation felt like heavy perfume had engulfed us. I had told them about Hasse, why he had written the work and how special it was to his patron, his wife and the Dresden court, but this was the first time they were hearing his music. Curiosity was high.

All eyes were glued on me. I took a deep breath and cued the choir's first entrance. The majesty of the opening "Kyrie" was so overwhelming I stopped the rehearsal after several minutes. I needed time; we all needed time, to savor the magnitude of the moment, for we had just sung music not heard for over two hundred years.

Trying not to get too emotional, I thanked the choir for their commitment to this project, to the tour and to Hasse. But I wasn't fooling anyone. My voice choked and tears began to flow. They knew what this moment meant to me. Did they agree Hasse's music deserved to be heard? Judging from the smiles on their faces and their moist cheeks, I sensed they did.

For the next two hours we sang through the entire score, marveling at the beauty of Hasse's writing. The choir's favorite movement by far was his rousing "Gloria," which I told them would include trumpets and timpani for even greater effect.

Hasse's ability to enhance the text, tell the story and create the mood was undeniable. Although most known for his operas, Hasse's love of the dramatic was equally present in his sacred music.

When I reminded the choir that they were going to sing the Mass in the very church for which it was written, they swelled with pride. They drank in the information like deer thirsting for water and sang each succeeding reading with even more fervor.

Hasse worked his same magic on everyone at the dress rehearsal. I had previously read through the Mass with the orchestra and the soloists, but this rehearsal, just days before the premiere concert, was the first time any of us heard the work in its entirety.

The color of Hasse's orchestration, his use of strings, winds, trumpets and timpani, added another dimension to the work. The majestic "Kyrie," the jubilant "Gloria," the dramatic "Credo," the glorious "Sanctus" and the prayerful "Agnus Dei," combined to create a work of power, inspiration and reverence.

I was stunned by the final effect. Added to the dramatic choruses were the lyrical arias. Here was Hasse at his zenith—the solo voice. Our soloists were superb and artfully demonstrated Hasse's melodic genius.

At the conclusion of the rehearsal, all agreed Hasse was a composer whose time had come—a master on every level. He had come to life before our eyes. We felt privileged to witness his resurrection. But the verdict was still out on what the public would think.

Chapter Twenty-Three: Fruition

On the day of the Premiere Concert the headlines in the local paper blared "Hear History Being Made." The article went on to say, "the Camerata Singers, the Bach Festival Orchestra and soloists will premiere Johann Adolf Hasse's *Mass in D minor* (1751) rediscovered, realized and edited by Dr. David Wilson. Also on the program will be the hauntingly beautiful contemporary work *Lux Aeterna* by Los Angeles composer Morten Lauridsen."

The stage was set for a gala evening. The overflow audience that filled the church attested to the fact there was much interest in this concert.

I was as nervous as a school boy at his first recital when I stepped onto the podium and acknowledged the applause. As soon as I lifted my hands to begin, my nervousness began to dissipate. We had done everything possible to ensure the success of this important and historic concert. Could we live up to the expectations? I knew we would, and the look on the choir's faces reinforced my expectations.

The effect of the Mass on the audience was just as I had hoped. At the conclusion of the final chord, the audience leaped to their feet in appreciation and honored the performers with many curtain calls. I could not stop beaming as I bowed to the choir and to the audience. During the intermission the buzz of excitement was everywhere.

The lights dimmed, signaling the start of the second half. In contrast to Hasse's music, Lauridsen's piece set a different mood. A master of lyrical vocal lines and achingly beautiful harmonies, his *Lux Aeterna* engulfed the audience in musical textures and hypnotizing colors. Coupled with rich organ registrations, the chant-like choral lines rose to triumphant climaxes and fell to hushed pianissimos.

Lauridsen is a singer's composer. His mastery of the voice is evident everywhere in this work. The choir loved singing his masterpiece. I could tell by their passionate reading of the score how honored they felt to be the ones to introduce this profound work to European audiences.

As the final "Amen" faded into silence, the audience sat stunned, not wanting to break the spell masterfully created by my dear colleague's music. In appreciation, I acknowledged his presence in the audience. The applause erupted. He joined us to take well deserved bows. Gesturing to the performers, he thanked them for their magnificent performance. A humble and gracious man, we felt his spirit fill the room. The audience responded with shouts of acclamation.

The evening was a triumph and the local papers proclaimed it so. Everything was now in place for our tour just months away.

The final concerts of the season featured the other tour repertoire. In May we produced a Renaissance Revelry, billed as "The spirit of Chapel, Court and Country comes to life in this Ode to Opulence—a Royal Fest with costumed singers, period instruments and delicious desserts." A good time was had by all, especially the singers, who let down their hair and sang and danced with gusto to the shawms, recorders and sackbuts of the Renaissance band.

We ended the season in June with two fund raisers. The headlines this time read, "The Camerata Singers Go International! In honor of their inaugural five-city European Concert Tour, the Camerata Singers of Long Beach preview works spanning five centuries that will be part of their concerts in Vienna, Prague, Leipzig, Dresden and Berlin." The purpose of these concerts was twofold: sing the entire program several times in public, and raise necessary scholarship funds. The concerts accomplished both goals.

The next few days were filled with behind the scene details necessary to ensure a successful tour. Several thousand programs in English, German and Czech were printed. Passports were registered with the tour company. Lists of what to pack and what to leave home were sent to the singers, along with instructions of when and where to meet at the airport.

☙ ☙ ☙

The sun rose clear and bright on June 17 as I climbed into the Supper Shuttle awaiting me. I pinched myself. Step one of the trip I had been looking forward to for decades.

Forty minutes later I entered Bradley Terminal at the Los Angeles International Airport and looked around to find my group. I didn't recognize anyone. I panicked. Where were they? The instructions said we would be met by our tour rep. Where was she?

I spotted a sign which calmed my fears—*Camerata Singers Check-In at Counter 5*. Our tour rep had done a superb job making sure all details were taken care of before we boarded the giant 747 flying first to London, then on to Vienna.

Just as I was about to take my seat on the plane, a cheerful flight attendant gestured to me. Is something wrong, I wondered?

"Please accept this token of thanks for booking your tour with us," she whispered in my ear as she ushered me to a seat in First Class. I was stunned. I had always flown coach. I had no idea what to expect.

No sooner had I had fastened my seat belt when the steward brought me a drink and some hors d'oeuvres, even before we left the terminal. If this was any indication of First Class service, I was happy to be spoiled.

At first, I felt a little guilty leaving my trusted companions back in Coach. As soon as I tasted a sip of Champagne, all guilt dissolved like the bubbles rising in my glass. I leaned back, took another sip and relaxed.

The plane landed at London Heathrow after the most pleasurable flight I've ever experienced. To say I was wined and dined is an understatement. Oh to be rich and travel that way all the time!

The hour layover gave me time to stretch my legs and receive some razing from the choir before re-boarding for the final leg of the journey.

After landing at the Vienna Airport, passing through customs, and collecting our luggage, we boarded our home for the next two weeks—a sleek, ultra-plush, double-decker coach complete with restroom, fridge and plenty of room to stretch out.

The bus whisked us away to our hotel in the center of the city not far from the *Ringstrasse*. I was back in my magic city where I started almost thirty years ago.

While many went out for a night on the town, I retreated to my room to rest and collect my thoughts. I knew from past experience concert tours were not a vacation for me. It was my responsibility to ensure its success, which only came from meticulous planning.

No sooner had I closed my eyes when I heard a rap on the door. I opened it and there stood our guide Gabi, the perky young woman from the Nuremburg office who met our plane at the airport. For the next two weeks she would be our eyes, ears and voice. Her responsibility was to make everything run smoothly, iron out the wrinkles, and take care of last minute challenges. Mine was to concentrate on the music. She had the schedule for the next few days and wanted to go over it with me.

Day 1: Morning bus tour of the city; lunch at the *Ratskeller*, followed by a rehearsal at the *Schottenkirche*, site of the first concert; evening free.

Day 2: Sing at a mass honoring a retiring priest, followed by Concert #1; attend a reception hosted by the Austrian Arts Council; visit to the wine country in the hills outside of the city for an evening of local food, music and entertainment.

Day 3: Morning free for shopping and sightseeing; afternoon guided tour of *Schoenbrunn* Palace and visit to the village of Eisenstadt; evening free.

The schedule she outlined looked fine to me, just the right amount of planned activity and free time for exploring and sightseeing. I thanked her for the detailed itinerary and ushered her out of the room. Closing the door I plopped down on the bed. I was so tired I could no longer keep my eyes open. My planning would have to wait.

The sound of church bells and smell of coffee woke me the next morning. My roommate, who was already up, had made a fresh pot which enticed me out from under the warm coverlet. He had gone for a walk so I had the room to myself. I used the time to organize my day, collect my scores, plan the rehearsal, shower and get dressed.

Not a big morning eater, I skipped breakfast, but nevertheless went downstairs to the main dining room to mingle with the choir. They were enjoying a typical Austrian breakfast, complete with eggs, sausage, potatoes, pastries, fruit, and coffee. The room buzzed with excitement as they related last night's experiences.

I left the hotel with Derek, our gifted accompanist, and went to the *Schottenkirche*, the site of our first concert. We needed time to check out the organ and the acoustics of this historic church.

From a distance, the church was an impressive site—a three story Basilica designed in the high Baroque style. Founded in the 12th century by Scottish-Benedictine Monks, it had been destroyed and rebuilt many times in its eight hundred year history.

Inside was even more impressive—the nave awash in shimmering gold and white, an imposing high altar, and a ceiling emblazoned with swarms of cherubs encircling the saints. Famous as the site for Haydn's memorial service at which Mozart's *Requiem* was performed, I was humbled to know we would give our first concert in this sacred and historic setting.

Derek and I climbed flights of stairs to the choir loft where a charming middle-aged woman welcomed us. As the church organist for twenty years, she helped Derek with the organ registrations while I selected the repertoire for the mass and subsequent concert.

After lunch, the choir arrived. I could hear gasps of amazement as they entered the massive church. Once assembled in the choir loft, three stories above the main floor, I announced the order of the music and the rehearsal began. The opening measures of Thompson's *Alleluia* left us all in amazement. With a five to six second reverberation, the blend and balance of the choir was superb. Miraculously, in that vast space our forty voice ensemble sounded more like four hundred.

"Don't push or over-sing," I admonished. "Let the room do the work. In these acoustics you can sing the softest pianissimos and be heard."

After the rehearsal, some went on a walking tour with Gabi, but I dashed to the opera house to get a ticket for the evening performance of Wagner's *Lohengrin*, an opera I was eager to see. I purchased a standing room ticket and joined the line in front of the opera house. Standing room is first come first served. I knew the routine. While living in Vienna during those months before moving to Portland, Cami and I went to the opera as often as we could arrange child care.

The production was brilliant. The cast, orchestra, sets, costumes, superb. I pinched myself as I stood in back of the dress circle so thankful to be back in this magnificent city again.

More rested and rejuvenated from the long flight, I boarded the bus the next day, which whisked us to the church for our first concert. The men in tuxes and women in long black gowns appeared nervous and excited at the same time. But I was confident. I knew how talented and well prepared they were.

The solemnity of the service for the retiring priest proved the perfect setting for the sacred music I planned for the tour. In his short homily, the priest commented on the beauty of our singing. We beamed with pride.

Even though most of the over-flow congregation could not see us perched high above, it was obvious the music was inspiring, as the majority chose to stay to hear our concert which immediately followed the service.

We opened the concert with Lauridsen's *Lux Aeterna*, ever mindful it was the European premiere of this much loved work. The acoustics were perfect, and the mystical interweaving of the organ and voices left little doubt to all that they were hearing a 20th century masterpiece.

At the conclusion of the concert, the audience erupted in applause, with many standing to try to see us high above them. The church organist was so impressed she asked if I would send her a copy of Lauridsen's piece. Anticipating this response from conductors and singers I knew I would be meeting, I had brought extra scores with me and gave her one. She was all smiles.

The next day was magical in a different way. Upon arriving at the little village of Eisenstadt where Haydn was composer in residence for the wealthy Esterhazy family for most of his life, we first visited the church where he was buried. As a symbol of respect, I asked the choir to gather in the small chapel around his tomb. With great reverence, for they had sung many Haydn masterworks, we sang Lutkin's *The Lord Bless You and Keep You*, the peaceful benediction I chose to end all our concerts. Others, who were visiting the church at the time, gathered around us in silence. They appeared to be as moved as we were by this serendipitous experience.

A short walk from the church was the imposing Esterhazy Palace. Because word had preceded us that we were on a concert tour, I was greeted by the curator at the entrance to the Palace. He asked if we would like to sing in the *Grand Saale*, the concert hall where Haydn performed much of his music. Honored by his request, I informed the choir of the invitation. Would they like to sing? "Yes," was their immediate answer.

185

We were ushered into a large wood paneled hall that resembled a ballroom more than a concert hall. From the raised stage at the far end of the room we sang an impromptu concert for those assembled. What a humbling experience. I had chills as I realized what music these hallowed walls have heard.

This unique experience reminded me that performing in historical sites, like the Esterhazy Palace, is one of the reasons concert tours such as ours can be life changing. We come not as tourists, but as ambassadors. We bring the gift of music, which in fact is a double gift, one for the singer and one for the listener. This realization was true every time we spontaneously burst into song. As a crowd gathered around to listen to our impromptu concert, we felt an intangible pride as we shared our talents with our new friends.

Until now the weather was perfect, warm and sunny. But when I awoke the next day it was cold and drizzling, a good day to travel. The six hour trip to Prague was quiet and relaxing. Many on the bus chose to rest up for the busy days ahead.

This time there was no drama at the border, so unlike when I ventured behind the Iron Curtain almost thirty years ago.

After checking into the hotel, we boarded the vessel *Pragerschiff* for a sunset dinner cruise, the perfect way to end a long day of travel. The view of the spires of the old city etched upon the grey clouds as the sun set was breathtaking. Many cameras flashed in hopes of capturing this magical moment on film.

Our concert the next day was in historic St. Nicholas Church in the center of the old city. Famous for its connection with the Hussites, the 16th century Czech Reformationists who were burned as heretics, the church was an impressive site. The bus pulled in front to let us out. Dressed in formal tuxes and concert gowns, our presence in the square caused many heads to turn.

Even more decorated and elaborate than the church in Vienna, the interior of St. Nicholas resembled an art gallery more than a church. Paintings and statues occupied every space.

We sang the first part of the concert from the gilded organ loft high above in the back of the narrow nave, and the second part downstairs in front of the main altar. At last we could see the faces of the large crowd gathered for our afternoon concert. The experience was electrifying.

While singing the final benediction, many in the audience wept. We knew we had made a connection. Our music had touched them.

Nymburk, a 13th century village sixty miles from Prague, was our next stop. It proved to be just as memorable. On the drive into town we saw posters advertising our concert tacked to doors and lamp posts. We felt welcomed.

Unbeknownst to me, we were part of a festival. Choirs from all over Europe had been invited to this little town to celebrate the music they were forbidden to sing during the communist occupation. "The Festival of Sacred Music," as it is known since the fall of the wall, was first a local event. Once the Russian's left the Czech Republic, the Festival grew in scope and now attracted choirs and audiences from around the globe.

The medieval walled town was not damaged physically by the war, but it certainly was damaged psychologically. Deprived of religious services for decades, the Festival celebrated the town's enduring faith and new freedom. Our program of sacred works from Renaissance to modern would be perfect for this concert.

This was confirmed later when I learned we had been awarded "First Prize" and received the coveted Golden Medallion for the best performance of the month-long festival.

The site of the concert was St. Giles Church. On the outside, a simple Gothic structure of multi-colored stone. Inside, the vaulted arches and gilded altar piece urged the eye upward to the feast of saints painted on the ceiling.

As I mounted the rickety steps to the organ loft for part one of the concert, I was able to steal a glimpse of the overflow crowd. Unlike our other concerts where the audience was more reserved, each piece was greeted with enthusiastic applause.

To begin the second part, the choir processed into the church singing, then formed a circle around the audience. The effect was spellbinding. The expression on the faces of the singers as they stood in the midst of the audience was transforming. The audience was equally enthralled judging from the thunderous applause.

For this most appreciative audience we sang every piece we knew, including all the spirituals. As we closed the concert with our traditional benediction, there wasn't a dry eye in the house, including mine. The choir sang magnificently. I was so proud to stand before them. The mayor presented me with a medal and a bouquet of flowers, then invited all to a reception in the city hall.

The warmth and generosity of the townspeople was apparent everywhere. Huge platters of local delicacies were passed around and much wine was consumed by all. We had adopted the people of Nymburk. I think they adopted us too.

The next day, a beautiful warm sunny morning, we left for Leipzig. My stomach tightened as I thought of all that had to be accomplished in such a short time.

The drive through the rolling green hills and thick forested valleys was reminiscent of the infamous train ride I took years ago when I first traveled through this area. However, this time, instead of seeing dilapidated farm houses and run down train stations, I saw evidence everywhere of the prosperity and renewed hope blossoming in this newly independent country. Several trains passed by—smiling faces and children's noses pressed against the glass, eagerly surveying the beauty of the countryside. I felt I had come full circle.

As soon as we arrived in Leipzig, I checked into my room and then took a walk around the old city, the city of Bach. I entered his historic *Thomaskirche* and was shocked by what I saw. It looked nothing like the simple interior of Bach's famous church I had seen in books and photos. Instead, huge sheets of plastic covered the walls, and scaffolding climbed up to the ceiling in front of the communion table, all in preparation for "Bach 2000," the 250th anniversary of the death of the town's most famous citizen. Leipzig was expecting hundreds of thousands of visitors from around the world to come pay homage to the greatest composer of all time.

Would Dresden be just as excited about Hasse's 300th anniversary, I wondered? From the lack of correspondence from city officials, I knew no such celebration was being planned, in spite of my many attempts to create interest. Maybe after our visit, someone will take notice. Someday, I prayed, Dresden will come to recognize their long neglected 18th century musical genius.

Dinner was at the *Auerbachkeller*, famous for its association with the poet Goethe. But I was not hungry. I was too nervous. My thoughts were elsewhere. Tonight was the first rehearsal with the *Pauliner Barock-*

ensemble, the orchestra we contracted for our Leipzig and Dresden concerts. The thought of what was at stake left my stomach in knots.

Gabi sensed how nervous I was and accompanied me to the *Peterskirche*, site of our concert. Now converted into a concert hall, complete with a choral shell and seated risers, in Bach's day St. Peter's was one of the four churches he was in charge of.

The orchestra was assembled and tuning when I walked into the hall. While Gabi introduced me, I looked into their faces and was surprised by how young they were. Most I guessed were in their mid-twenties or early thirties.

They applauded politely as I mounted the podium for our first reading of the Hasse Mass. In my halting German I tried to convey the importance of this concert, how personal it was, and how much I appreciated their support of the project.

With those few remarks I gave the downbeat and the Hasse magic happened. As promised by their director, they were an excellent ensemble, and soon I realized I had nothing to worry about. My stomach relaxed. My confidence returned. They read through the Mass with ease, and after the break, with equal success, the Bach cantata. Well versed in the Baroque style, the orchestra responded to my every comment and suggestion. Being so young, many of the players had grown up under communist rule and had little contact with outsiders. Our collaboration was their first experience with Americans. They were as nervous as I about the venture. After the initial rehearsal, we all relaxed.

The concert was sponsored by the Leipzig University Choir, who acted as hosts and producers. They were so efficient I had little to worry about. I didn't have to set up, move a chair or a music stand. Unlike the concerts I produced back home, all I had to do was conduct. What a luxury to be so well taken care of. I loved it.

The next day was a full one—two rehearsals and an evening concert. During the morning rehearsal we worked on the Hasse Mass. As it had been awhile since the choir had sung the work with orchestra, I wasn't sure how easily it would come together. But again my fears were allayed. They breezed through the reading.

The afternoon rehearsal was a bit more challenging. Bach's Cantata is difficult and required more rehearsal time. But at last everything came together. I excused the choir and spent the remaining time working with the soloists.

All was now ready for one of the most important concerts of the tour. We were daring to perform Bach in Leipzig, his spiritual home. Was I being naïve? I would soon find out. I wasn't worried about the reception to Hasse, for no one knew his music. But I imagined the audience knew every note of the Cantata. Would we be judged by the highest standards of a very critical audience? "Hasse in Dresden," I was confident. But "Bach in Leipzig?" I had my doubts.

As the orchestra tuned, the choir took their places on the seated risers. The buzz of anticipation from the large audience, which came to hear this choir that had journeyed all the way from Long Beach to Leipzig, was noticeable. I had a lump in my throat as I gestured to the performers to rise and acknowledge the warm applause.

The men dressed in formal black tuxes, and the women in elegant black gowns with matching sequined blouses, were a handsome and distinguished sight. The director of the Leipzig University Choir made a few opening remarks to the audience and then turned to the choir. With the help of Gabi to translate, he expressed his profound thanks to us for coming to Leipzig and for bringing the healing gift of music. Acknowledging that few in the audience had been to our country, he was most grateful we had come to his.

I thanked him for his kind remarks and then told the audience, again with Gabi's help, about the work they were about to hear, emphasizing the relationship between Bach and Hasse, and the fact the work had not been heard for over two hundred years. Upon hearing my short discourse, a hush fell over the room.

The soloists took their seats. I shook hands with the concertmaster, motioned to the choir to stand, took a deep breath and gave the downbeat. I was so nervous I don't remember conducting the first few measures. After the orchestra introduction, the choir entered. The sheer beauty of their sound soon calmed my fears. Every eye was glued on me. They were focused. I felt in complete control. They gave me confidence to go beyond the heights we had achieved in rehearsal. The orchestra sensed it too, and responded to my every gesture.

What a joy to make music, and such inspiring music, with so many talented and dedicated musicians. Judging from the long sustained applause after the last notes died away, the audience confirmed my belief—Hasse was a musical genius. All the work it took to bring his music back to life was well worth it.

After the intermission, the performers entered the concert hall to thunderous applause. So far we had won them over. Would they be as generous after hearing our Bach? The Cantata began with a plaintive overture followed by an opening chorus of pleading souls. The text taken from the Psalms projects a pensive and penitential mood. Part Two, on the other hand, is taken from Revelations and leads from despair to a triumphant conclusion with the text "Worthy is the Lamb that was slain," the same text Handel used at the conclusion of his great masterpiece, *Messiah*. With the addition of trumpets and timpani the effect was brilliant. Bach proved to be a master at word painting. I choose this Cantata for that very reason; it was a perfect foil to Hasse's liturgical work. The effect worked. The audience burst into applause as soon as the last "Amen" reverberated throughout the hall.

At the after-concert reception sponsored by our hosts, the comments from the audience were full of praise. They loved our Hasse and our Bach! Now, there was only one more hurdle to cross before my dream would be realized.

Chapter Twenty-Four: Fulfillment

The day at last arrived. "D Day." The day I had been anticipating for three decades—performing Hasse's Mass in Dresden in the church for which it was written. With hopes so high I doubted it would be possible to live up to my expectations.

The short drive from Leipzig to Dresden gave little time for reflection. No sooner had we boarded the bus and said goodbye to our gracious hosts in Leipzig when we pulled up in front of our ultra-modern hotel not far from the center of the old city.

I glimpsed the roofline of the *Zwinger* Palace as I embarked from the bus and wanted to kneel down and kiss the ground. So much had changed since my last visit. Everywhere I looked was evidence of the rebirth of this historic city. Like Hasse, Dresden too was rising from the ashes.

The schedule for the day was packed and time was of the essence. After lunch we were to rehearse for a couple of hours, go back to the hotel to rest and have dinner, followed by a 7:00 concert in the *Hofkirche*, Hasse's church. Although the other concerts were important, tonight's was the one I had been dreamed of for over thirty years. Not surprisingly, I was a nervous wreck.

But then I soon learned it was not to be.

As I entered the hotel, a representative from the Dresden tour agency, who helped set up this part of the itinerary, gave me shocking news. The renovation of the *Hofkirche* was behind schedule and was not open to the public. I slumped down in a chair and buried my head in my hands. We had come so far, sacrificed so much, planned so carefully.

I knew the church was being restored, but had been assured it would be completed well before our visit. What had gone wrong? I could have scheduled the tour a month later had I any idea it might not be finished.

I was heart-sick as the weight of the news sank in; my dream, like Hasse's reputation, had vanished into thin air.

"Are you telling me the concert has been canceled?" I blurted out, trying not to show both my grief and anger.

"No, not at all," reassured the tour agent. "We have procured another venue for you, and the concert is scheduled for tonight as planned."

"Will anyone be there? How will people know? Why wasn't I told of this sooner?" I had so many questions; I hardly listened to the explanations given to me.

She knew there was a possibility the church would be unavailable, but kept hoping with each day good news would arrive. Not until we landed in Vienna was the official edict issued—the church was closed for an indefinite period of time.

Gabi put her hand on my shoulder to comfort me. She knew how upset I was and how much this concert meant to me.

"I made the decision," she said in an apologetic tone. "I didn't want to give you the disappointing news until we arrived in Dresden, knowing there was nothing anyone could do about it," she said with tears forming. "You can blame me for not telling you sooner."

I grabbed her hand. "I don't blame you Gabi," trying to give both of us some comfort. My anger was directed elsewhere. I knew she was right; there was nothing I or anyone could do about it. It was just lousy timing.

"You made the right decision," I told her. "I would have obsessed about it. My disappointment may have affected the other concerts. You were right not telling me earlier. So where do we go from here?"

The agent stepped in. "The concert will be held in the *Kreuzkirche*, one of Dresden's most revered churches. Located in the *Altmarkt*, the center of the old city, the church has an illustrious history. Martin Luther preached here, as has every other prominent theologian."

I don't need a history lesson just now, I thought, but listened politely while trying to collect my thoughts.

"The weekly demonstrations held in the *Kreuzkirche*, which grew from a few dozen to tens of thousands, helped bring the wall down in 1989." She was beginning to convince me.

"The *Kreuzkirche* is much beloved by the citizens of Dresden. I can assure you there will be throngs of people who will come to hear your concert."

When she mentioned the *Altmarkt*, I flashed back to my visit when I saw much of the city in ruins. Was this the same square where I bought the record of Bach's *B minor Mass* recorded by the choir of the *Kreuzkirche*? Didn't I peek inside the church as they were clearing out the rubble from the crumbling roof? I was sure it was. Maybe I had come full circle in spite of all my plans and this was where I was supposed to conduct.

As soon as Gabi told me the news, she went over to the choir who by now had gathered in the lobby and were wondering why I looked so despondent. I heard groans as they too registered their disappointment. Several came over to comfort me. True to Camerata spirit, they assured me the choir was committed to making this concert the highlight of the tour, in spite of the set back.

After checking into the hotel, the bus took us to the new concert site. We embarked and nervously climbed the steps, not sure what we would find.

When I entered the massive church I was overcome, not by its opulence, for none could be seen, but by its simplicity. Plain drab stucco walls, a single stone altar and hard wooden benches dominated the vast interior purposely left unadorned after its destruction in 1945.

As I walked down the center aisle, Gabi told me more of its history. During the occupation, this was the only church allowed to hold religious services. People of all faiths gathered here to worship. The *Kreuzkirche*, The Church of the Holy Cross, was the spiritual home of the people of Dresden. Although the *Hofkirche* was more resplendent, it represented the aristocracy, the privileged, not the humble spirituality of the commoner. If I wanted to reach the people and bring Hasse to Dresden, this was the right place.

Her wise words from one so young, but from one who had experienced oppression and want for much of her life, struck a chord deep inside me. I knew she was right. We were where we were supposed to be.

The choir helped set up the chairs and music stands for the rehearsal, and soon the orchestra arrived. To set the right tone, I asked to Gabi to repeat what she had told me. The looks of disappointment turned to

194

understanding smiles as she relayed to the choir the importance of this great edifice.

After those calming remarks, I launched into the rehearsal, quickly finding the acoustics of the space dictated slower tempos than I had planned. Much like the challenges Hasse faced in the *Hofkirche*, the reverberation and resulting echo greatly affected the sound. The clarity of line we had worked so hard to create was obliterated.

Once I adjusted to new slower tempos, the rehearsal went smoother, and I dismissed the choir so I could spend more time with the soloists. In order to fill the space, they had to sing with a fuller, more focused tone. But being true professionals, this did not prove to be a problem. All was in place now for the most important concert of the tour.

At ten to seven the choir filed into the church and took their seats. The orchestra tuned, and the senior minister rose to address the large assembled audience.

"Tonight is an historic occasion for our city. The Camerata Singers have come all the way from Long Beach, California to perform the music you are about to hear—music by one of our own, music not heard in our city for hundreds of years. If it hadn't been for their efforts we might never have had this opportunity. The conductor found Johann Adolf Hasse's music by ignoring restraints put upon him, by braving the Iron Curtain, by persevering, much like we had to do for all those years. What he and the choir bring tonight is a gift, and we are privileged to be present to receive it. Please help me welcome the Camerata Singers of Long Beach, the *Leipzig Pauliner Barockensemble*, and their conductor Dr. David Wilson."

Upon hearing those heart-felt words the audience rose to their feet and expressed their approval.

Do I remember much of the concert? Not really. I was too emotional. As I turned the pages of the score and conducted my beloved singers, I realized my dream was becoming a reality. We were in Dresden. We had brought Hasse back to his city. The Mass I found thirty years ago was coming to life in the city he loved. I had so many to thank—Drs. Short, Bodley, Decker, Hamm, Novak, Reich, my family and all the people who believed in me and my dream.

At the conclusion of the concert, I bowed to the choir, and with grateful tears in my eyes reminded myself that it wasn't about the place, it was about the music. It had always been about the music.

Coda

Like all good stories, there is often a postscript, and in my case I chose to call it a coda; just after you think the piece is over, the composer adds another ending. So it is with my story. There is another ending.

After the triumphant concert at the *Kreuzkirche*, we went back to the hotel to celebrate. During the revelry, I heard someone trying to get our attention by clinking on a champagne glass. It was Gabi. She had an important announcement.

"Attention everyone, attention," she shouted over the joyous din.

"Tomorrow morning before you board the bus, be sure to have your music handy." The room buzzed with excitement. "I have a surprise for you, but won't say any more about it now." The buzz grew even louder as rumors flew.

With much anticipation and a feeling of great accomplishment, I arose the next morning, packed, and boarded the bus for the journey to Berlin, the last stop on our tour.

"Have your music handy," Gabi again reminded us with a hint of glee in her voice. "We have one more concert to give before we leave Dresden."

Completely baffled, I had no idea what she was planning.

We had not traveled five minutes when the bus stopped and Gabi told us to get off. When I looked out the window my heart stopped. The bus was parked in front of the *Zwinger* Palace. Were we going to sing here, the site of so many of Hasse performances?

"Follow me," she said. To my surprise we did not mount the steps to the Palace, instead we continued down the street. Suddenly, I saw the *Hofkirche* in all its restored glory. Surmounted with huge statues of the saints and a golden cross on its tallest spire, it looked just like the picture

197

on the cover of our program—a reproduction of a famous 18th century print—a picture I had carried in my head and heart for all those years.

We entered through a back door which had been left open for us and stepped inside. Yes, there was scaffolding and ladders and men in hard hats busily putting the finishing touches on the walls and ceiling, but through the clutter I could see the glory and majesty of this royal church.

"Please watch your step and gather over here in the pews to the left of the altar," Gabi said with a lilt in her voice, for she knew what a gift she was about to give us.

Sensing my disappointment the day we arrived in Dresden, Gabi had made special arrangements for us. We were going to give a concert in Hasse's church after all. Not for masses of people, just for us, the ones for whom it meant so much.

With a pride difficult to put into words, I stood in front of my beloved choir.

"Form a circle and let's begin our concert with the piece you often sang surrounding the audience—Mendelssohn's *Heilig*—only this time we will sing it for ourselves."

The music I heard, that we all heard when their voices began to swell, was miraculous. Clear, ringing, warm, spacious, all the adjectives which describe beautiful choral singing—it was all there and more.

The minute the workman heard us they stopped and put town their tools. We did have an audience after all, but that wasn't important. This concert was for us. We sang the music we had grown to love, ending with Randall Thompson's *Alleluia*, the piece that had nurtured and inspired me throughout my life.

At the conclusion of our mini-concert, the men clapped. Out of the crowd gathered around stepped a man who introduced himself as the architect for the project. He had been up on a scaffold and came down when he heard the music, curious to see what this was all about. When Gabi explained to him and the workers the significance of this impromptu concert, they clapped even louder.

Luckily, I had a CD of the Hasse concert we performed in March. I reached into my bag and handed it to him. Studying the cover, he saw the 18th century print of the *Hofkichre*.

"Now I know why this church is so special to you," he remarked as he held up the CD for his men to see.

Walking over to one of the workmen, he whispered in his ear. A minute later the man reappeared and handed something to the architect, who, placing it in my hand, said, "Please accept this stone as a token of our thanks. You have reminded us of the true importance of this church."

I was overcome. It was a stone that had broken off from a pillar that had held up the ceiling of the church, a stone that had heard Hasse's music at the dedication hundreds of years ago, a stone that had witnessed history.

The last piece of the puzzle was finally in place. I had brought a token of Hasse back to his beloved church and left with a treasured souvenir. The cycle was complete, my dream fulfilled.

And yes, it wasn't about the place, it was about the music. It had always been about the music.

DAVID WILSON, teacher, scholar and conductor, is Professor Emeritus of the Thornton School of Music at the University of Southern California. In addition, he is Artistic Director/Conductor Emeritus of the Long Beach Bach Festival and the Camerata Singers of Long Beach.

A graduate of the University of the Pacific and University of Illinois, he also studied conducting at the Berkshire Music Festival in Tanglewood, and the Hochschule für Musik in Vienna.

As a recognized expert in 18th century music, Dr. Wilson has conducted hundreds of works of Bach, Handel and their contemporaries. His rediscovery of the sacred works of Johann Adolf Hasse is the subject of his first book.

David can be contacted at: djwilsonauthor.com

Selected Photographs

College of Pacific Professor Virginia Short and
her 1962 European Tour Group

Dr. J. Russell Bodley, Dean of the Conservatory,
University of the Pacific

Courtesy of the Holt-Atherton Special Collections
University of the Pacific Library

Dr. Harold Decker, Chairman of the Choral Music
Department, University of Illinois, Urbana

Courtesy of the University of Illinois Archives, Faculty and
Staff Press Release File, RS 39/1/11

Dr. Leopold Nowak, Director of Music Collections
Nationalbibliothek, Vienna

The author in front of the Dresden Library

Dr. Wolfgang Reich
Director of Music Collections
Sächsishche Landesbibliothek, Dresden

The Dresden Hofkirche as the author saw it in 1971

The author in front of the Zwinger in Dresden.

A fragment of the Kyrie from the Dresden manuscript
of Hasse's Mass in d minor, 1751.

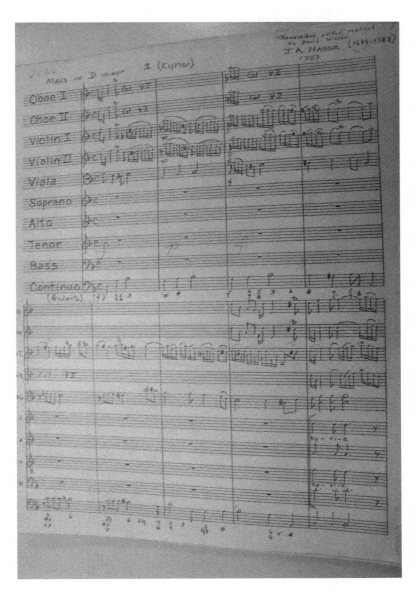

The author's edition of the Kyrie from the Mass in D minor, 1751

Portrait of Johann Adolf Hasse, circa 1748

Portrait of the young Faustina Bordoni, circa 1735

Portrait of the young couple Johann and Faustina, circa 1735

Giovanni Antonio Canaletto's painting of the Hofkirche, circa 1748

LONG BEACH, KALIFORNIEN

EUROPA TOURNEE
WIEN, PRAG, NYMBURK, LEIPZIG, DRESDEN, BERLIN
17. JUNI – 1. JULI 1999

Cover of the 1999 Camerata Singers of Long Beach
European Concert Tour Program

Camerata Singers accepting applause after the concert
in Nymburk, Czech Republic

Rehearsal before the concert in the Peterskirche, Leipzig

The pastor of the Kreutzkirche, Dresden, introducing
the conductor of the Camerata Singers

The restored Hofkirche, June 1999

The author conducting the Camerata Singers
in an impromptu concert in the Hofkirche

The restored interior of the nave of the Hofkirche, Dresden

KONZERT

Camerata Singers of Long Beach
Los Angeles, USA
Pauliner Barockensemble, Leipzig
Dirigent: Dr. David Wilson

Hyun Joo Kim – Sopran	Sharon Swaney Tanabe – Alt
Bong Won Kye – Tenor	James Bessey – Bass

Derek Gordon - Continuo

Messe in D Moll   **J. A. Hasse**
Kantate 21 (BWV 21)   **J. S. Bach**

Kreuzkirche Dresden
Sonntag, 27. Juni 1999
19.00 Uhr

SPENDENSAMMLUNG ZUGUNSTEN
DER INNENERNEUERUNG DER KREUZKIRCHE

Poster advertising the Dresden concert
of the Camerata Singers of Long Beach

A monument honoring Hasse's birthplace in Bergedorf, Germany

CPSIA information can be obtained
at www.ICGtesting.com
Printed in the USA
FSHW021502280319
56672FS